BUSINE$$ OFFENSE

BUSINE$$
OFFENSE

How to Win with People, Process, and Technology

BRIAN BENTON

WESTBOW
PRESS®
A DIVISION OF THOMAS NELSON
& ZONDERVAN

Copyright © 2018 Brian Benton.

All rights reserved. No part of this book may be used or reproduced by any means, graphic, electronic, or mechanical, including photocopying, recording, taping or by any information storage retrieval system without the written permission of the author except in the case of brief quotations embodied in critical articles and reviews.

WestBow Press books may be ordered through booksellers or by contacting:

WestBow Press
A Division of Thomas Nelson & Zondervan
1663 Liberty Drive
Bloomington, IN 47403
www.westbowpress.com
1 (866) 928-1240

Because of the dynamic nature of the Internet, any web addresses or links contained in this book may have changed since publication and may no longer be valid. The views expressed in this work are solely those of the author and do not necessarily reflect the views of the publisher, and the publisher hereby disclaims any responsibility for them.

Any people depicted in stock imagery provided by Thinkstock are models, and such images are being used for illustrative purposes only. Certain stock imagery © Thinkstock.

Scripture quotations taken from the New American Standard Bible® (NASB), Copyright © 1960, 1962, 1963, 1968, 1971, 1972, 1973, 1975, 1977, 1995 by The Lockman Foundation Used by permission. www.Lockman.org

Scripture quotations are from the ESV® Bible (The Holy Bible, English Standard Version®), copyright © 2001 by Crossway, a publishing ministry of Good News Publishers. Used by permission. All rights reserved.

Scriptures taken from the Holy Bible, New International Version®, NIV®. Copyright © 1973, 1978, 1984, 2011 by Biblica, Inc.™ Used by permission of Zondervan. All rights reserved worldwide. www.zondervan.com The "NIV" and "New International Version" are trademarks registered in the United States Patent and Trademark Office by Biblica, Inc.™

This book is a work of non-fiction. Unless otherwise noted, the author and the publisher make no explicit guarantees as to the accuracy of the information contained in this book and in some cases, names of people and places have been altered to protect their privacy.

ISBN: 978-1-9736-1434-0 (sc)
ISBN: 978-1-9736-1436-4 (hc)
ISBN: 978-1-9736-1435-7 (e)

Library of Congress Control Number: 2018900498

Print information available on the last page.

WestBow Press rev. date: 03/20/2018

CONTENTS

About the Author vii
Preface ix
Introduction xi
Chapter 1 Relationships 1
Chapter 2 Leadership 14
Chapter 3 Purpose 23
Chapter 4 Values 25
Chapter 5 Vision 29
Chapter 6 Strategy 32
Chapter 7 Focus 40
Chapter 8 Superpower 44
Chapter 9 Lead Gen 49
Chapter 10 Sales 58
Chapter 11 Scale 67
Chapter 12 Cybersecurity 81
Chapter 13 Technology Road Map 96
Chapter 14 Binary 106

ABOUT THE AUTHOR

Brian Benton is a Jesus follower, husband and father. He is the author of The Hurry Up No Huddle Life Offense and founder of Xccelero, Inc. a Managed IT Service Provider. He has served as a lay youth pastor for middle school students and a life group leader for New Life Church. Benton has a Bachelor's Degree from Middle Tennessee State University.

PREFACE

My sweet mother, Kathy Benton, recommended I wait until I got married before I wrote my next book, which allowed me to focus on building and multiplying a family. I married my beautiful wife, Christy Benton, on May 29, 2016, and instantly became a stepfather to Mark Wesley Smith. We obeyed the command in the Bible to, "Be fruitful and multiply" (Genesis 1:28), and in a couple of months, my wife discovered she was pregnant. We were blessed with a healthy baby boy named Maverick Wyatt Benton, who was born on February 21, 2017. As I was writing this book, my wife discovered she was pregnant again, so I felt compelled to finish the book before Malone Whitley Benton was born.

INTRODUCTION

In Business Offense, I will help you develop a playbook for people, process, and technology so you can multiply the growth of your business. Business Offense appeals not only to business leaders but also to anyone interested in multiplying the growth of their organization.

Visit businessoffense.com for tools and resources as well as information on training and coaching programs.

FUNDAMENTALS

The fundamentals of the business offense are purpose, values, strategy, and vision.

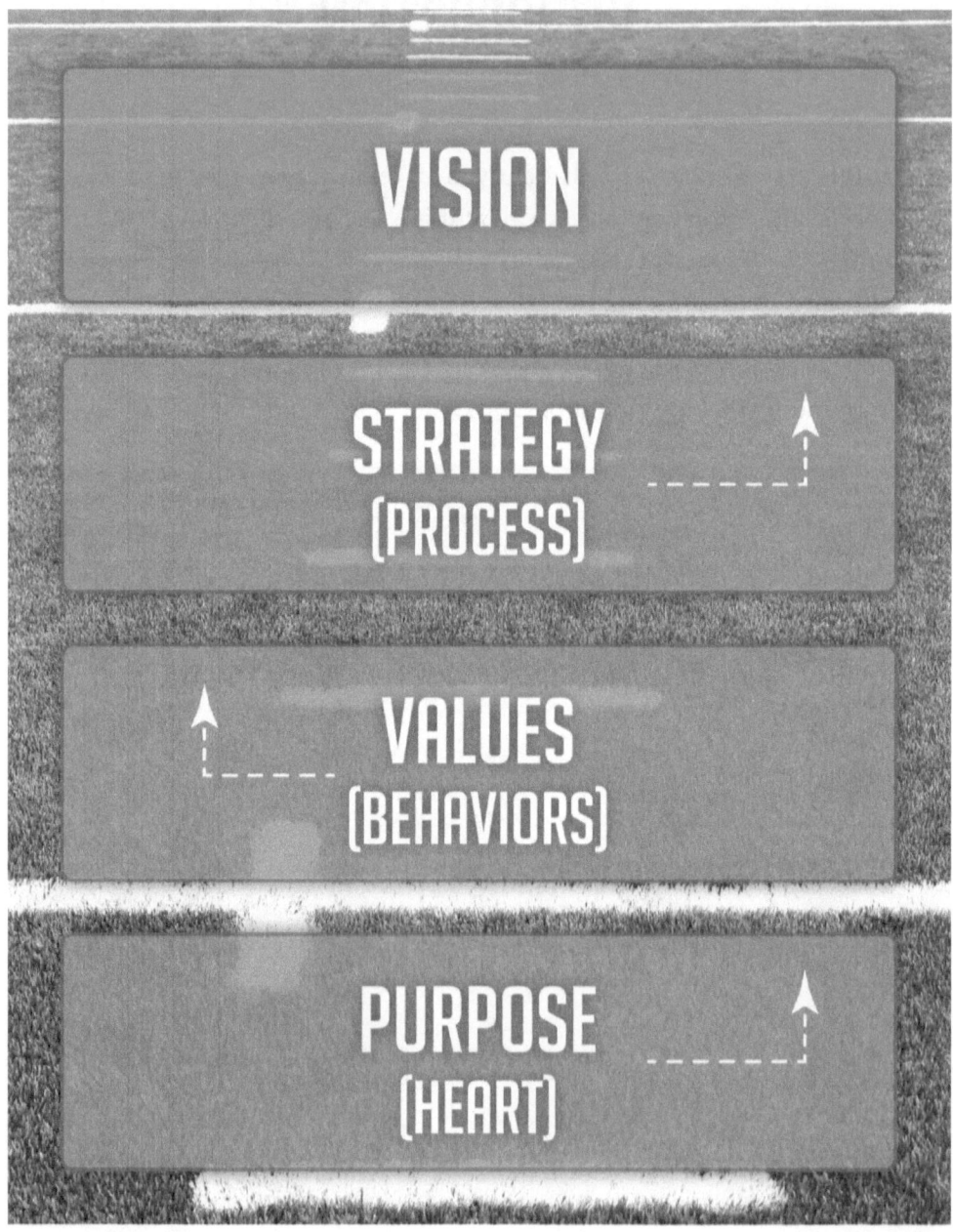

Business Offense Process

GAME PLAN WORKSHEET

The business offense game plan worksheet helps your business visualize the most important things to multiply the growth of your business.

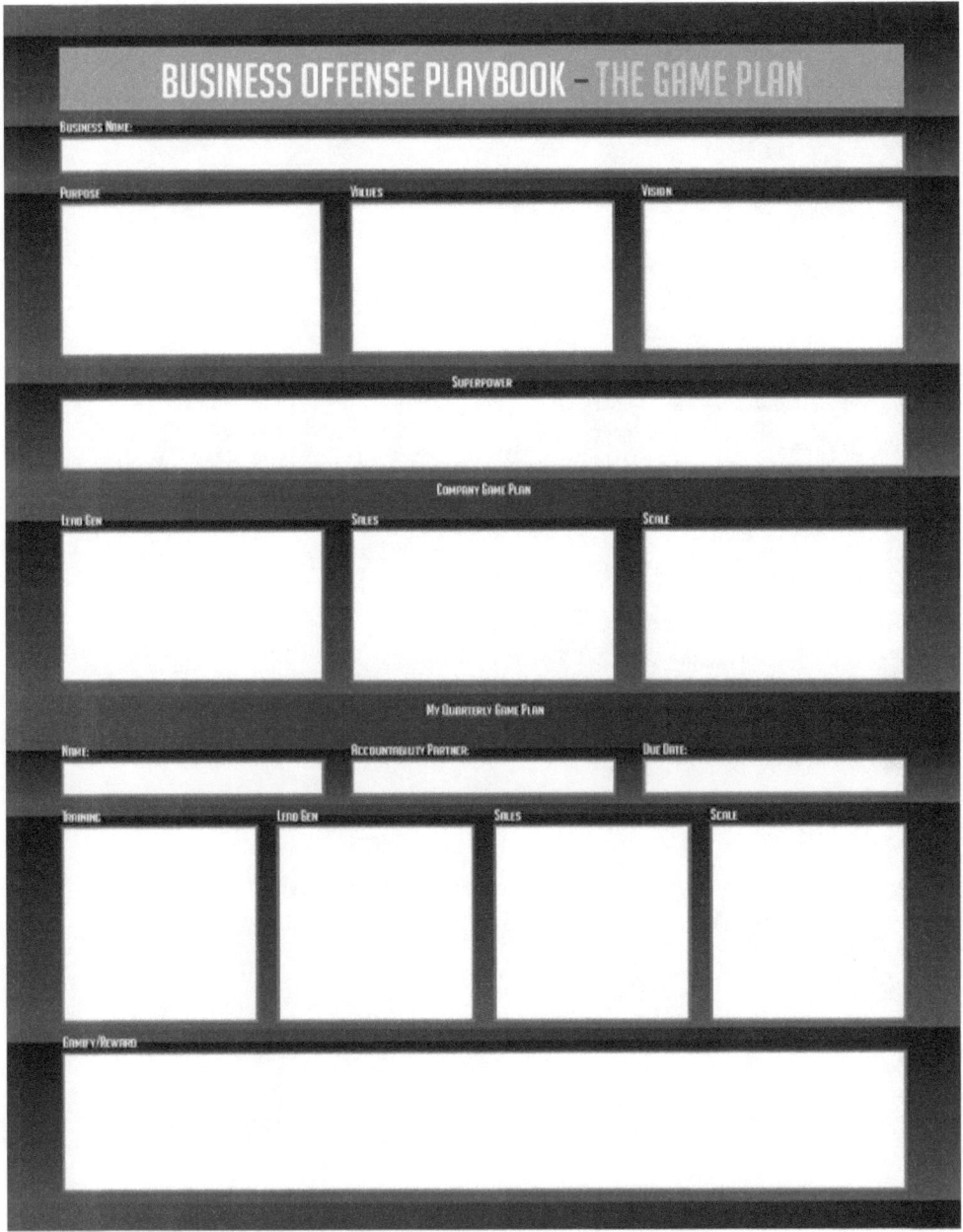

Business Offense Game Plan Worksheet

GAME PLAN ADJUSTMENTS

The business offense game plan must be adjusted every quarter to continue to compete in the fast-paced business world.

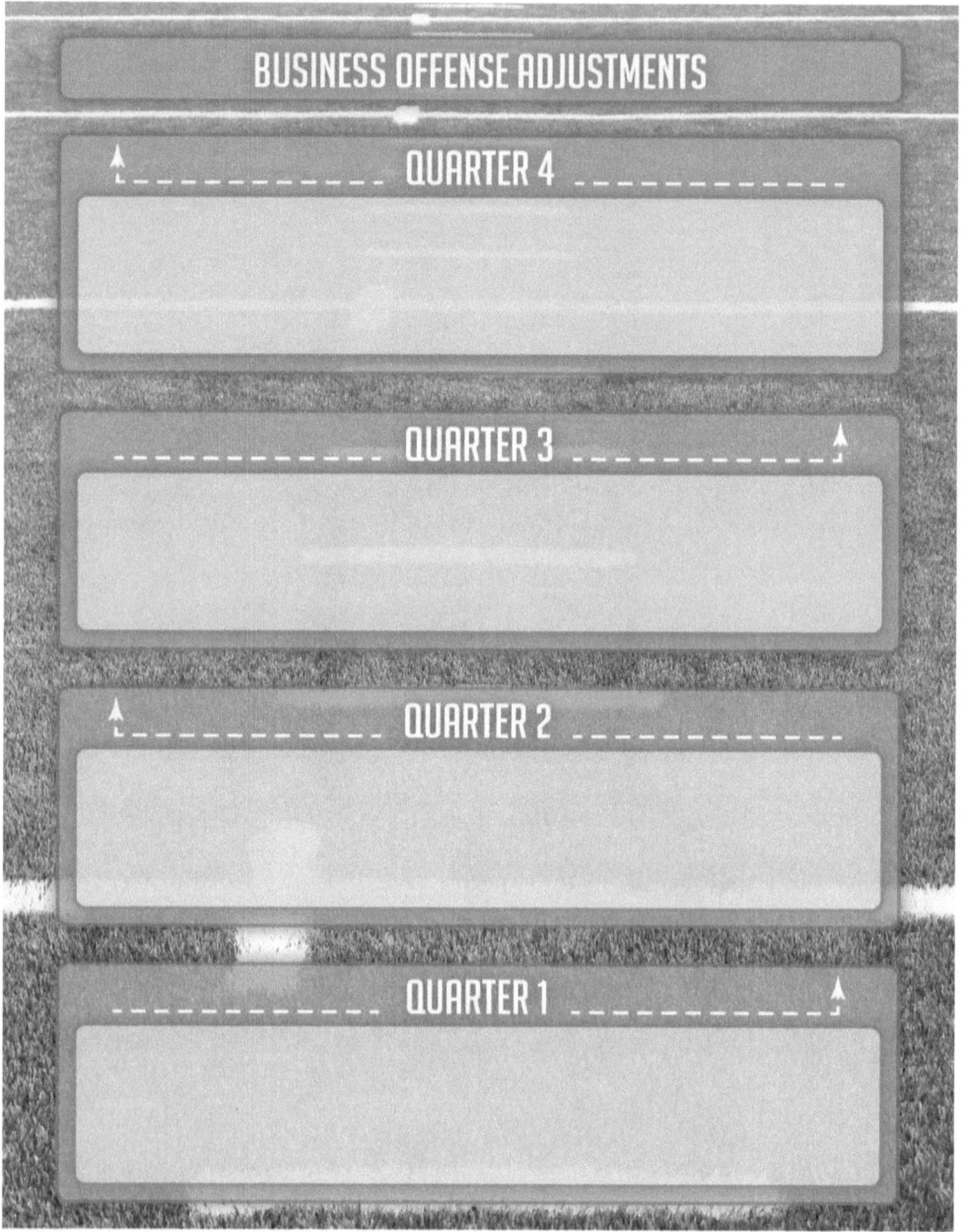

Business Offense Game Plan Adjustments Process

GAME PLAN ADJUSTMENTS WORKSHEET

The business offense game plan adjustments worksheet helps your business visualize the most important things to adjust every quarter to compete in the fast-paced business world and multiply the growth of your business.

Business Offense Game Plan Adjustments Worksheet

CHAPTER 1
RELATIONSHIPS

He must increase, but I must decrease.
—*John 3:30 (NASB)*

THE MOST IMPORTANT RELATIONSHIP

I'm sure you would agree you were created when your mom and dad came together in the act of knocking boots, which is also known as the act of procreation. I use the term act of procreation because the terms lovemaking and sex in our society typically only refer to the pleasure aspect instead of the complete purpose of sex.

You may be wondering, What does this have to do with growing a business? Everything! The last time I checked, you need people to work in your business and buy your products, so people procreating is good for business. The reason I mentioned that is to highlight this important point: I believe that all human beings ever created through the act of procreation were born through Adam and Eve.

Why do I believe this? The book of Genesis tells us God created humans in His image and likeness (Genesis 1:27). He formed man from the dust of the earth and then breathed the breath of life into the nostrils of Adam (Genesis 2:7).

God is so powerful that He only needed to breathe the breath of life one time to create every human who has ever lived and will ever live. Chew on that thought for a few moments, and then you might take a ten-minute praise break to thank God for how awesome, powerful, and wonderful He is. Back to the story in Genesis, God saw it was not good for Adam to be alone, so he created a helpmate, Eve, by putting Adam to sleep and taking a bone from his rib (Genesis 2:18–25). God established that He cares about not only our vertical relationship with Him but also our horizontal relationships.

The concept of multiplication and growth was not invented by humans but was invented and ordained by God. Check out what the word of God says.

> God blessed them; and God said to them, "Be fruitful and multiply, and fill the earth, and subdue it; and rule over the fish of the sea and over the birds of the sky and over every living thing that moves on the earth." (Genesis 1:28 NASB)

God created Adam and Eve in His image and likeness to be fruitful and multiply to rule over and care for the earth. Adam and Eve created children who created children who populated and are still populating the earth. Every human being who has ever lived is an image bearer of the God of the universe. Wow!

Since we were created by God for a purpose, do you think your most important relationship should be your vertical relationship with the Creator and Boss of the universe?

I hope your answer is yes.

What's so amazing about God is when you know Him, you will understand you not only have a vertical relationship with Him but also a horizontal relationship with Him. The only way to have a relationship with God is placing your faith and trust in Jesus. Why is He the only way? God's intent was for Adam and Eve to choose to remain innocent in the garden and not be aware of evil, because God is good. God allowed them to eat from every tree in the garden except the tree of knowledge of good and evil, delegated authority to them, and encouraged them to have lots of sex!

In the garden of Eden, Adam and Eve disobeyed the one thing

that God told them not to do: eat from the tree of knowledge of good and evil (Genesis 2:16-17). God said, "You surely will die" (if you eat the fruit). What did God mean? He meant that their physical bodies would eventually die due to the wages of sin, which is disobeying God.

When Eve ate the fruit, she placed her trust in what Satan said instead of placing her trust in what the Creator said (Genesis 3:4). She was tempted by the lust of her flesh, lust of her eyes, and pride of life (Genesis 3:6). When Adam ate the fruit, he placed his trust in what Eve said instead of placing his trust in what the Creator said (Genesis 3:17). Both Adam and Eve failed to trust God because of their lack of faith.

Now you may be wondering, If God is God, He must know everything, including that Adam and Eve would be deceived, eat the fruit, and be punished. Yes, He already knew that would happen. God foreknew that He would create angels and a third of them would chose not to worship Him, but He still created them. God foreknew that Adam and Eve would fail to trust Him by disobeying the one command in the garden of Eden but still trusted them to be fruitful and multiply and to rule and care for the garden.

Adam and Eve became aware of good and evil, thus losing their innocence when they ate the fruit. They realized they were naked and sewed fig leaves together to cover themselves (Genesis 3:7). Both Adam and Eve tried to cover up and hide their sin from God, but God already knew they would sin, knew where they would hide, and knew He would implement justice for their disobedience. God issued the justice then demonstrates His grace is bigger than sin: "He made garments of skin for Adam and his wife and clothed them" (Genesis 3:21). The text doesn't say how He made the garments of skin, but I believe it was Jesus preincarnate who killed an animal, skinned the animal, and then clothed Adam and Eve with the skins as a picture of His grace that would cover our sins by the blood He would shed on the cross. In the old covenant, God required man to atone for the sins by the blood of an animal (Leviticus 17:11) as a foreshadow of Jesus, the Lamb of God, paying the ultimate sacrifice with His blood (John 1:29) for the sins of everyone who believes (Acts 13:39).

Offensive Strategy
- Who is Jesus to you?

HORIZONTAL RELATIONSHIPS

I established the importance of our vertical relationship with God because our relationship with God has a direct impact on our horizontal relationships with our fellow humans. The first four of the Ten Commandments are based on our vertical relationship with God, and the last six are based on our horizontal relationships with our fellow humans. I caught this principle after hearing Pastor Rick Bezet of New Life Church teaching on the Ten Commandments. In the New Testament, Jesus simplified the first four commandments (vertical relationship) in Matthew 22:37–38 when He said, "Love the Lord your God with all your heart and with all your soul and with all your mind. This is the great and foremost commandment." Jesus simplified the last six commandments (horizontal relationships) in Matthew 22:39, when He said, "The second is like it, 'You shall love your neighbor as yourself.'"

What is interesting about the gospel is that we learn that our vertical relationship becomes both vertical and horizontal when we become believers in Christ. In John 15, the Bible describes Jesus as the Vine and his followers as the branches. This doesn't resemble a top-down model of multiplication but an organization model that grows from the inside out horizontally. Think for a minute of how a vine grows. The branches grow out from the vine horizontally, and the fruit is produced on the branch but flows from the vine.

As followers of Jesus, we believe the fruit flows from Jesus through us to fulfill His vision and purpose. If we look at leadership from a horizontal model instead of top-down, we can open the potential for greater multiplication, which is how Jesus intended the kingdom of God to multiply. In the garden of Eden, the plan for Adam and Eve was to be fruitful and multiply and fill the earth. Parents would teach children to worship the Lord. When the children become adults, they would be fruitful and multiply and teach their children to worship the Lord.

In the New Testament, Jesus reaffirms the plan from the beginning with the Great Commandments and Great Commission. The plan includes vision, strategy, values, and purpose: love God, love people, and multiply the kingdom of God. As mentioned earlier in this chapter, Jesus simplified the last six commands of the Ten Commandments when He said, "Love your neighbor as yourself." (Matthew 22:39) The last six commands are about our horizontal relationships with our fellow humans, which is what we will focus on in this chapter.

During a leadership retreat, my pastor, Cory Cangelosi, taught us a process to hold ourselves accountable to pray for and invest time with the people we are raising up in our ministries by drawing a table like the one shown below. You can draw the table on a notepad, whiteboard, fillable PDF, or whatever works best for you. In the top row, you enter the person's name and place a check mark under "Prayed For?" "Called?" and "Invested Time?" each time you completed that action. On the second row, you enter the cell phone number of the person, prayer requests, answered prayers, and the next step in building him or her up. I believe this process can positively impact all your horizontal relationships.

Name	Prayed For?	Called?	Invested Time?
Cell Phone	Prayer Requests	Answered Prayers	Next Step

FAMILY

The second-most-important relationship in your life is your spouse, and the third-most-important relationship is with your children. We live in a very busy culture with high demands for work performance, endless distractions, and opportunities to be entertained 24–7, but life moves by too fast to miss out on the opportunity to invest time with your family. Your business may fail, you may be laid off or fired, or you may have a disability or sickness that might prevent you from work.

We are not promised tomorrow, so we need to make the most of every opportunity we have with our family. It's so easy to justify in our minds that working extra hours is necessary to provide for our family. Providing for your family means more than just tangible material things but also includes intangible things that will have more impact on the lives of your family. How many items in your lifetime will you purchase and throw away? In America, I would guess at least hundreds but more than likely thousands. We can always replace tangible things with other tangible things, but we can't replace the intangible things, like time we invest in our family, creating memories with our family, and having fun with our family.

Offensive Strategy

- Do you invest more in the priorities outside of your home than the priorities in your home?

IRON

The fourth-most-important relationship in your life is to have an accountability partnership. The Bible uses the phrase iron sharpens iron in Proverbs 27:17 to illustrate the purpose of an accountability partner to sharpen you. You cannot sharpen yourself with an accountability partner who is soft. The way a biblical accountability partnership should work is that both people sharpen each other by holding each other accountable, speaking truth in love, encouraging each other, and challenging each other to grow. The accountability partners in my life have had a huge impact on my success and growth. In my first book, The Hurry Up No Huddle Life Offense, I developed the concept of IRON MAN:

Inspired	Inspired to live for Christ
Reflect	Reflect the life of Christ so He is glorified
On guard	Be on guard against the enemy and always be ready for battle
Nurture	Learn from a mentor and serve as a mentor
Motivate	Motivate and encourage each other
Account	Account to God for your actions and hold each other accountable with love
Never quit	Christ never gave up on us, so never give up on Christ

Offensive Strategy
- Do you invest time surrounding yourself with iron?

CHURCH

The purpose of the church is to multiply the kingdom of God, build up the body of Christ, and serve as the hands and feet of Jesus to Glorify God. The purpose of a church home is to have a place you regularly attend to corporately worship, listen to the word, fellowship, and encourage each other to do the what the word says.

Offensive Strategy:
- Do you invest time serving at a local church?

FRIENDS

We all need friends in our lives to do life with. Your friends may fit into any one of the categories mentioned in this chapter.

Offensive Strategy
- Do you have fun with your friends?

COMMUNITY

We have a vested interest in the sustainability and future of our communities, which is why we should be involved in our communities.

The first step in building relationships is to get to know your neighbors and learn the social-economic components of the community. The second step is to find ways to serve the community.

Offensive Strategy:
- Do you invest in a process to build relationships with your neighbors and serve your community?

GOVERNMENT

The first step in building a relationship with the government is to obey the laws except when the law tries to supersede the word of God. The second step is to pay your taxes. The third step is to pray for government officials at the local, state, and federal level. The fourth step is to build relationships with government officials. Most large companies have dedicated roles that all they do is manage relationships with government officials because the decisions made at the local, state, or federal level can have a positive or negative impact on business. If large companies make a commitment to invest in government relationships, I think it's a good idea for everyone. The fifth step in the process is to vote and contribute to the political process to have a voice in the direction of your city, state, and country.

Offensive Strategy
- Do you invest in a process to build relationships with government officials?
- Do you pray for all levels of government leaders to make wise, godly decisions?

TEAM

One of our guiding principles at my first Managed Service Provider, "If we take care of our people, our people will take care of our clients, and our clients will take care of our cash flow." This is a cliché that everyone understands, but I personally like simplicity, so I made it a guiding principle to keep me accountable to focus on caring for the people first before the results. The results of a business come from a combination of people, process, and technology, but it starts with people. The best way to help your people succeed is to serve them by equipping and empowering them with the best tools, resources, and training and reward them with generous praise and incentives based on their performance.

Offensive Strategy
- Do you invest in a process to build up your team with the best tools, resources, training, and incentives?

CLIENTS

Your clients pay you money to keep you in business, will refer your business if you do a good job (net promoter score), and can be the first to implement your new product or services. It's a lot harder to get a new client than to keep an existing client, so you need an account management process to invest time with your current clients face to face in addition to voice and digital communications. You should treat managing your relationship with your current client like earning the business of a new client. That will keep you hungry to continue to earn the business. Otherwise you may get lazy in the process and assume your clients will continue to do business with you.

Now just like not everyone maybe a good fit for your team, the same is true for clients. Some clients might not be a good fit for your product or your services even though you like cash money. As business owners, we want to hear that cash register sound, cha-ching, cha-ching, cha-ching, as the revenue pours in, but not all revenue is good revenue.

You may have clients who cost you more than the revenue they are providing you in return for your products and services. You should include as part of your account management process to assess whether keeping the client is worth the time, effort, and resources or if you should part ways with the client. This is not fun, but it's part of business. To move forward in your business, you may have to let go of clients.

Offensive Strategy
- Do you invest in a process to build relationships with your clients?

POWER BASE

Most businesses come from word of mouth referrals, so it's not always what you know but who you know. Your power base are people you know you can help or they can help you. The first step in building your power base is to list everyone you know. The second step is to identify the industry they have expertise in. The third step is to identify if you can help them or they can help you. The final step is to develop an action plan to cultivate the relationship at least once every three months. In your database, you should include the following information:
- Name and contact information
- Industry
- Hobbies and interest
- Skills and education
- Church and community service
- Last contact date/note

The best way to cultivate a relationship with your power base is to send them a lead/referral, connect with them over coffee or lunch, or send them a praise note with gift card.

Offensive Strategy
- Do you invest in a process to build relationships with your power base?

TALENT BASE

Your talent base are people you want to mentor or possibly hire for future opportunities. Most smart business owners, leaders, coaches, principals, and pastors recruit and maintain a list of people they want to hire to maintain a deep bench and avoid costly hiring mistakes. The best way to avoid hiring people for a job they are not a good fit for is to get to know them relationally, which helps you understand their

character, competency, and ability to fit in your organization. I keep the following information updated in my talent base in my CRM. You can use OneNote, Evernote, Google Docs, or whatever works best for you.
- Name and contact information
- Hobbies and interest
- Skills and education
- Work History
- Church and community service
- Last contact date/note

The purpose of maintaining the talent base is to hold yourself accountable to cultivate the relationships for future opportunities. If you are mentoring someone, you may want to cultivate the relationships on a weekly or monthly basis.

Offensive Strategy
- Do you invest in a process to build relationships with your talent base?

CENTERS OF INFLUENCE

Business is about relationships and more about who you know than what you know. Centers of influence (COIs) are movers and shakers in the community who have influence in industries you serve with your business. Establishing relationship with COIs in industries you serve takes time, money, and resources but can reap a harvest for your business if you commit to the process of investing in building your COI relationships.

The first step in the process is to identify potential COIs, determine what value you can give to them in terms of help, business, or leads, and then ask them for a meeting so you can present the value. The second step is to continue to plant seeds of value in the relationship so they view you as a producer rather than a consumer. The third step is to ask the COI to help you gain new business. Essentially, you want to build a partnership, with both parties wanting each other to succeed.

Offensive Strategy
- Do you invest in a process to build relationships with your COIs?

PROSPECTS

A prospect is a business, organization, or individual you may want to do business with but you are not sure if they are a good fit. Prospecting is the process of identifying which prospects are a good fit for your business model. Most organizations use a sales funnel process to sift out the prospects similar to how a gold miner would sift for gold. In business, not all relationships are meant to be, so it's important to sift out the prospects that are not a good fit to avoid pain later after entering into an agreement.

Offensive Strategy
- Do you invest in a process to prospect for new clients?

VENDORS

A vendor is a business you purchase products and services from to use in your business or resell as a product or service to your clients. In our modern society, we've rewired our brains in how we interact with vendors. We access the vendor's website via the internet, search for a product, click on a button to order the product, and receive the product without speaking to any humans in the process. This process is great when everything works but can be a pain when there is a breakdown in the process. You call for support and are transferred multiple times, which I call the call transfer circle of pain. It's painful to invest an hour to get a resolution that takes five minutes. I think it's still best practice to partner with a vendor that respects your time, values you as a customer, and supports you with an account management team to help you better serve your clients.

Offensive Strategy
- Do you partner with a vendor that respects your time, values you as a customer, and supports you with an account management team?

COMPETITORS

In business and life, there are winners and losers. You are going to win business and lose business. I wish I was always able to win, but that's not the reality of the world. Some people would rather crush their competition like a grape instead of investing time to build relationships with competitors for the mutual benefit of the industry or industries they serve. I think it is wise to stay humble and build relationships with competitors to sharpen each other and build up the industry or industries you serve. If you are smart with the relationship, you both can find ways to win!

Offensive Strategy
- Do you invest in a process to build relationships with competitors to improve the industry you serve?

CHAPTER 2
LEADERSHIP

The king's heart is like channels of water in the hand
of the Lord; He turns it wherever He wishes.
—*Proverbs 21:1 (NASB)*

WHY DO BUSINESSES FAIL?

Money, money, money, money, money, money, money, money, money, money ... There is no doubt that it takes money to stay in business and grow, but money takes away from what is most important: leadership, leadership, leadership, leadership, leadership, leadership, leadership, leadership, leadership, leadership ... I repeated it ten times to drive the point home, which is what all good leaders should do. Leaders can drive a business to fail with no compelling vision, poor time management, poor planning, and no differentiation, but ultimately it is a result of poor processes.

WHY DO BUSINESSES SUCCEED?

Businesses succeed when leaders make an all-in commitment to focus on the processes that are the most important to a business:
1. Set the purpose and values of the organization and then live the purpose and values.
    - Why: People want to follow a leader who is real and sincere, not a phony baloney.

2. Create a compelling vision, invest in the vision, and sell the vision.
   - Why: People want to believe they are a part of something greater than themselves.
3. Build a team of wise counselors to develop a strategy to generate leads, convert leads, scale operations, and differentiate the products and services.
   - Why: Read Proverbs 15:22.
4. Multiply their leadership influence throughout the organization with a process of leaders developing leaders to execute the strategy, believe in the vision, and live the purpose and values.
   - Why: Leaders take responsibility to get results.

I wrote a separate chapter to focus on each area: purpose, values, vision, and strategy in this book. The purpose of this chapter is to focus on the power of influence and the impact influence has on the process of leaders developing leaders. The process of leaders developing leaders unlocks the potential to multiply the growth of your business.

THE POWER OF INFLUENCE

The greatest example of the power of influence to multiply the growth of an organization is the example of Jesus. Jesus asked ordinary people to follow Him to become fishers of men (Matthew 4:19) and empowered them to do extraordinary things. Jesus focused on developing twelve disciples as part of His plan to multiply His kingdom. Jesus sent out His disciples two by two (Mark 6:7) because two are stronger than one (Ecclesiastes 4:9). Jesus's strategy to multiply His kingdom by sending out disciples in pairs resembles the concept in the garden of Eden of Adam and Eve multiplying their family.

In the New Testament, we learn that human marriage is actually a reflection of Christ marrying the church. The purpose of a human marriage is for a man and woman to unify as one flesh to multiply and then lead their children so they grow up to get married as one flesh to multiply and then lead their children. The purpose of the church is to unify together under Christ's leadership to multiply the kingdom of God throughout the earth. In the Great Commission, Jesus commands all believers to go and make disciples in all of creation (Matthew 28:16–20). I finally caught this principle by witnessing how it works at New Life Church. The purpose of making disciples is to multiply the kingdom of God. The math of the multiplication is simple. Two disciples make two disciples, and thus you have four disciples. Four disciples make four disciples, and thus you have eight disciples. Eight disciples make sixteen disciples, and the multiplication continues to happen.

The multiplication growth is exponential because followers of Christ lead non-believers to Christ, who become disciples and lead non-believers to Christ. From generation to generation, Jesus's followers have preached and are still preaching the gospel message all over the earth while facing persecution, oppression, death, sickness, and disease.

The key to the multiplication and growth of your business or organization is developing a process of leaders building leaders, just like God's plan for building His church. Whatever role you have, everybody is a leader. You're a leader in your home. If you are a husband, you are the leader of your wife and kids. If you are a wife, you are a leader of your children. If you are the big brother or sister, you can lead your younger siblings. You're a leader in your business. You're a leader in the community.

My point is that everyone with influence can lead. If you have one friend, you have influence to lead your one friend. If you have a managed service business, you have engineers, architects, and network administrators who all have influence to lead customers to implement the right solutions to deliver end results that positively impact their business.

Kirk Cousins, Redskins quarterback, citing his faith, turned down a $53 million long-term contract, opting for a one-year contract as reported in the Christian Post article on July 24, 2017. Kirk mentioned he wanted to be more than a leader on the football field but a man who can lead others to Christ. Kirk understands the essence of leadership is influence: "I do think naturally I am a leader. I believe that leadership at the end of the day is influence," he said. "I think that more than anything as a Christian I want to be able to influence my teammates for Christ and that's not going to change."

In the traditional top-down organization, the title speaks directly to the influence the leader has over people in the organization. The top-down organization, if built correctly, has many advantages, including eliminating heads to execute and communicate faster, narrowing the focus of departments/teams, eliminating duplication, and overall simplifying the organization of the business. However, the top-down organization can fall into the trap of not developing a process of leader development from the bottom up, which can limit the full intellectual and leadership capability of an organization.

The impact your influence has on people is based on your conviction and reputation, not your title. Your passion fuels your conviction, which builds your reputation. Your conviction is the absolute certainty that you believe in what you are doing and your reputation certifies what you believe in by the actions you've taken over time. If you walk the walk and talk the talk, you will have great influence to lead people. If you are a fake and a snake, then the truth will eventually come out and you will lose your influence. Remember, your influence is only as strong as your reputation and conviction.

Let's examine the greatest example of how someone came from the top to empower a bottom-up revolution with the power of influence. By now, you've probably guessed who I would mention. Yes! You are right. Winner, winner, chicken dinner. If you guessed Jesus, give yourself a pat on the back. Jesus, the Son of God, left His rightful place in heaven to come to the earth to start a revolution by influencing people to follow Him.

Jesus practiced what He preached and didn't command or ask anyone to do anything He didn't do on earth. Jesus inspired His followers by loving them and setting the example on how to live. Jesus set the example of servant leadership by serving His disciples as He wants all His followers to serve. In John 13:5–17, Jesus washed the feet of his disciples even though the Father had given Him all things (all power in the universe). In Jewish culture, not even a Jewish slave would be expected to wash someone's feet, much less the host. Jesus hosted the disciples as His guests at the last supper but chose to humble Himself to wash their feet instead of delegating the task to a gentile slave, which was a common Jewish practice.

I don't know about you, but I've never had the desire to wash someone's else feet to serve them. First, I've seen some jacked-up feet and have smelled some nasty feet from several feet away that made me want to puke. By the way, I'm not perfect and have two pinky toes that look weird compared to my other toes and my feet stink, but not as bad as my wife's. Just kidding—my wife's feet always smell like roses. (My wife approved that message.)

Jesus's ministry on earth only lasted three years, but He continues to impact the world unlike any other religion with the process of making disciples. From generation to generation, Jesus's followers preach Christ crucified, risen from the grave, while facing persecution, death, disease, sickness, and poverty to lead people to Jesus so they become disciples.

The kingdom of God has this process of disciples making disciples:
- God is patient toward you to come to repentance (2 Peter 3:9)
- God invites you to become a disciple (Matthew 4:19–20) through faith by grace in Jesus (Ephesians 2:8–9).
- God will equip you to make disciples (2 Timothy 3:16–17).
- God will encourage you to make disciples (2 Timothy 1:7).
- God will empower you to make disciples (Ephesians 1:19–20).
- God's plan to multiply His kingdom is successful from generation to generation.

THE PROCESS OF LEADERS DEVELOPING LEADERS

Step 1. Identify potential leaders by looking at your employees and clients as potential leaders instead of followers. Why? Leaders can influence followers to become leaders. When a client becomes a leader for your business, he or she can influence other people to become your clients. This is the heart of word-of-mouth referrals.

When employees become leaders, they take more ownership to live the purpose and values, believe in the vision, execute the strategy, and influence prospects to become clients.

Let's study briefly how social media companies scale so fast. Facebook, Twitter, Snapchat, LinkedIn, and Google scaled fast because they essentially led "followers" to use their free cool platforms so that "followers" use the free cool platform to lead other "followers" to become "followers" on the platform, and the multiplication continues to occur. In a sense, social media companies developed a process of leadership throughout their platform. Obviously, there were large capital investments in people, process, and technology to scale social media, but the investors wouldn't have committed without the potential massive growth of users and opportunity for ad revenue.

So what do you look for when identifying people to become leaders? The four c's is a good place to start:
- Character (Will)
    - Do they have the conviction and reputation to influence people to follow them?
    - Are they teachable and willing to learn?
    - Are they willing to surround themselves with people who are smarter and wiser than they are?
    - Do they demonstrate a servant's heart, humility, passion, honor, and courage?
- Competency (Skill)
    - Do they have the potential to get the job done?
- Chemistry (Will and Skill)
    - Do they get along well with people?
- Calendar (Will)
    - Do they have the time to invest in becoming a leader?

Step 2. Remember to be patient with people. You can't put people in a microwave, zap them, and they become a leader. The process of developing leaders takes time because people grow incrementally over time. A baby learns how to roll over, then to crawl, then to walk, and then to run, which all takes time. The same is true for leaders. You don't give someone a position of leadership to lead a thousand people if he or she was unable to lead ten people.

You build up leaders to lead small groups and then lead larger groups and then lead larger groups. This concept comes directly from the Bible: "Whoever can be trusted with very little can also be trusted with much, and whoever is dishonest with very little will also be dishonest with much" (Luke 16:10 NIV).

In our fast-paced culture, we send a text message and expect a response immediately. We send an email message and expect a response immediately. We make a phone call and expect the person we are calling to answer the call on the first ring. We run a Google search to answer a question and expect to receive the answer in less than one second. We start a business and expect to be immediately profitable. We live in a digital society that expects immediate results, but that is not how human relationships work. Human relationships are analog, not digital.

Step 3. Recruit people to become leaders by simply asking them. You don't want to force anyone to become a leader but rather call it out of them so they buy in to the fact they can lead, but you must ask. If you ask and they say no, they may not be ready at the time, but if you believe they have the potential to lead, continue to invest in your relationship and ask again.

Step 4. Equip leaders to be successful:
- Set clear expectations.
- Release control.
- Define measurable stretch goals.
- Provide the tools and resources to get the job done.
- Provide continuous training opportunities.

Step 5. Encourage leaders to be successful:
- Follow up to make sure they have the tools, resources, and training to get the job done.
- Hold them accountable to meet the expectations and exceed the goals.

- Praise them publicly.
- Give generous incentives based on performance.

Step 6. Empower leaders to develop leaders:
- Train them on steps 1 through 5.
- Include developing new leaders as part of their goals.

Step 7. Repeat steps 1 through 6 to continue to multiply! You might be thinking, This all sounds great, but what happens when leaders fail? Easy—every leader will fail at something in his or her life, and it's a matter on how he or she rebounds from the failure. When leaders fail, you re-equip, encourage, and empower them to succeed in the future. Most successful leaders learn their best lessons from mistakes they make, which typically costs them time, resources, and relationships. Obviously, if there are character problems that cause the failure, the leader probably will need to step down or step out to heal and let the next leader to step up and move the business or organization forward.

Offensive Strategy
- Do you invest in the process of leaders developing leaders?

THE BEHAVIORS OF GREAT LEADERS
- Serve first.
- Focus on what's most important.
- Surround themselves with wise counsel and accountability.
- Stay hungry and reject mediocrity.
- Honor their word and honor people.
- Think big and act bold.
- Communicate, coordinate, and follow-up.
- Set clear expectations, roles, and responsibilities.
- Inspect what they expect.
- Help people realize and develop their God-given abilities.
- Equip and train their team.
- Always recruit.
- Build strong coalitions.

- Outsource non-core competencies.
- Eliminate duplication/redundancy.
- Practice what they preach.

Offensive Strategy
- Do you exhibit the behaviors of a great leader?

CHAPTER 3
PURPOSE

> Trust in the Lord with all your heart and do not lean on your own understanding. In all your ways acknowledge Him, And He will make your paths straight.
> —*Proverbs 3:5–6 (NASB)*

The purpose of every business is to generate revenue and make a profit. Hopefully you want to generate lots of revenue and make a healthy profit because it's good for your employees and clients. The more revenue you generate, the more people you can hire to deliver your products and services. The more profit you generate, the more capital you have available to reinvest in improving and growing your business.

Although every business shares the ultimate purpose of generating revenue and making a profit, every business is unique. A business needs a purpose statement to guide people to focus on why the business generates revenue and makes a profit.

The "why" or purpose of the business is essentially the heart of the business. The human heart pumps blood continuously in and out to all parts of the body. If the heart isn't functioning properly, the blood stops flowing and the body eventually dies.

The same is true for a business; the purpose is the heart of the business. When leaders stop living the purpose, the purpose doesn't flow in and out of employees to continue to generate revenue and make a profit. The purpose of the business could inspire people to come work with you if they believe they will receive economic, social and even spiritual shared value and connect to a movement greater than themselves that has a positive impact in the world.

The purpose of the Coca-Cola Company listed on their website as of July 4, 2017, states, "Our Roadmap starts with our mission, which is enduring. It declares our purpose as a company and serves as the standard against which we weigh our actions and decisions.

- To refresh the world …
- To inspire moments of optimism and happiness …
- To create value and make a difference."

The purpose of the Coca-Cola Company is written in a few short sentences to inspire people to buy their product and inspire people to work with Coca-Cola to connect with a movement greater than themselves that has a positive impact in the world.

In my Managed Service Provider, Xccelero, we align the technology strategy of a business with their vision, so writing the purpose statement was easy. The purpose of our business is to help businesses execute their vision with people, process, and technology. The success of our MSP business is directly related to the success of our clients executing their vision. When we help our clients execute their vision with people, process, and technology, we get to be a part of helping them execute their vision, which is very exciting and cool.

Offensive Strategy

- Does your purpose represent the "heart" of your business?

CHAPTER 4
VALUES

So, whether you eat or drink, or whatever
you do, do all to the glory of God.
—*1 Corinthians 10:31 (ESV)*

The values of a business are the standards of behavior on how to act in the world and drive company culture. When you develop a new building, you start by laying the foundation and then build on top of the foundation. The values of a business are like the foundation of the business. You start with the purpose of the business and then build on the values of the business. Without a strong foundation of values, the leadership won't have standards to build the business on and the business could crumble.

The most successful business and organizations keep their values between three to seven values. Typically, anything above seven values is hard for people to remember and for leaders to coach people on the values.

The Coca-Cola Company listed seven values on their website as to "serve as a compass for our actions and describe how we behave in the world.

- Leadership: The courage to shape a better future
- Collaboration: Leverage collective genius
- Integrity: Be real
- Accountability: If it is to be, it's up to me
- Passion: Committed in heart and mind

- Diversity: As inclusive as our brands
- Quality: What we do, we do well"

The first value listed at the top for The Coca-Cola Company is Leadership. If one of the most successful companies on planet earth recognizes leadership as the top value, it's probably a good idea to follow their lead. I wrote the chapter on leadership as the second chapter in this book because of how important it is to an organization. The other six values are important but not as important as leadership. By the way, before reading any further, please feel free to drink an ice-cold Coca-Cola product. If you are on a soda-free diet, don't worry—you can drink Dasani water.

In my first MSP business, Xccelero, we created seven values to build our business on:
- God first, family second, business third
- Servant leadership
- Passion
- Honor
- Courage
- Fun
- Generosity

In our business, God is first because we cannot breathe without God. We make God first not so it will guarantee our success but to focus on who created us and who we live for. We make our family the second priority because we only have one family in life. Our business may experience peaks and valleys or fail, but our family is constant in our life. For husbands, the priority is to love your wife like Christ loved the church and gave Himself up for her (Ephesians 5). For wives, the priority is to respect your husband (Ephesians 5). If you have children, your responsibility is to disciple your children in the ways of the Lord, so that they can lead their own families and become productive citizens who are not a burden in society but rather servant leaders who can help people.

We live in a very competitive fast-paced world, where we must continually improve to adapt to the current and future economies, so it's easy to want to make business a higher priority than God and family, but regardless of what happens, God is our priority and our families are our second priority.

The second value in our business is servant leadership. We believe the greatest model for leadership is the example of how Jesus served first and inspired followers to serve. Two thousand–plus years later, hundreds of millions of people still follow His leadership plan. We believe if we serve our team, they will serve our clients, and our clients will take care of our cash flow.

The third value in our business is passion. We stay hungry to live our purpose, live our values, and execute our vision.

The fourth value in our business is honor. We believe honor produces commitment, praise, accountability and integrity. We honor our word because we serve a God that honors His word. When we make a commitment, we honor that commitment. We honor our commitment to God. We honor our commitment to our families. We honor our commitment to our employees. We honor our commitment to our clients. We honor our commitment to our government. We honor our commitment to our partners. We honor our commitment to our community. We honor people by praising them and not gossiping about them. We are accountable in everything we do because we are honorable people. We maintain our integrity in everything we do because we are honorable people.

The fifth value in our business is courage. Courage is what you need to help you grow. You can't grow if you comfortable or scared. You can't grow if you don't admit your mistakes and grow from them. Some mistakes are more expensive than others, but it's part of business. You can't execute a vision that is overwhelming and bigger than what you think you can accomplish without courage. You must have courage to be willing to fail or experience rejection repeatedly. Most successful leaders and businesses fail, make mistakes, and are rejected repeatedly along the way on their path to success.

The sixth value in our business is fun. We believe if you make work fun, people will be excited to live the purpose, live the values, and execute the vision.

The seventh value in our business is generosity. We share the profits with our team and donate our time and resources to serve the communities we live in.

Offensive Strategy
- Are you building your business on values?

CHAPTER 5
VISION

> But seek first His kingdom and His righteousness,
> and all these things will be added to you.
> —Matthew 6:33 (NASB)

Everybody needs vision. Every team needs vision. Every business needs vision. You need to have a vision of where you're going in life and a vision where your business is going in the future. When I wrote this book, I had a vision to reach people with the gospel to multiply the kingdom of God and to inspire people to reach their God-given potential on the earth, including but not limited to multiplying their business with people, process, and technology.

Before we go any further discussing vision, I want to remind you that tomorrow is not promised. In James 4:13–17, the word of God tells us that we shouldn't boast about today or tomorrow because our life is like a vapor. That doesn't sound very encouraging and quite frankly slaps me in the face when I read it because I'm a big vision guy who wants to accomplish great things.

The passage of scripture keeps me humble to know that my life is like a vapor. I need to focus on what's most important and live life for God day by day. I can only boast in going all in to execute a vision if the Lord wills it to happen.

The vision of the business is the road map of where the business is going, Lord willing, in the future. You only have one life to live and can't go back in time, so why not go all in with a bold vision that inspires people to think big? If you're in the United States, in North America, or even in any first-world country, the opportunities that we have compared to the third world should give us no excuse to think big. It doesn't mean that you have to become a millionaire or billionaire, but it does mean you have opportunities to positively impact the world if you choose to take advantage of those opportunities.

When a real estate developer assesses land to build homes on, he or she sees the vision of what the properties will look like after the property has been built. He or she believes in the vision, sells the vision to investors, hires contractors to build the vision, and then sells the vision to home buyers. The real estate developer follows a process to create the vision, sell the vision, fund the vision, and execute the vision.

Step 1. What would your vision be if you had unlimited resources?
- The first constraint we may experience in creating a vision is that we limit the vision to the current resources available, but you must think in terms of your resources increasing over time as your business grows and people invest in your vision.
- The vision for this book is for it to sell one million copies and be available in all major languages. Go big or go home!

Step 2. Are you excited or even overwhelmed to execute the vision?
- If you are answered yes to the above question, then you are ready to move forward to step 3. If you answered no, your vision isn't big or bold enough to fuel your excitement.

Step 3. Have you written down your vision or illustrated your vision?
- If you are answered yes to the above question, then you are ready to move forward to step 4. If you answered no, you need to write down your vision or illustrate your vision in a graphic, PowerPoint, or video so you can "see it to believe it" and get excited about it!
- For example, the vision of the technology company ConnectWise in 2017 is to build a "single pane of glass" by using connectwise.com as the central hub for all of their products and services.

ConnectWise created a graphic to illustrate their vision so all their employees and partners could see the vision, believe in the vision, and buy into the vision.

Step 4. Can you sell the vision?
- A vision will not sell itself. You must sell the vision with certainty to your investors, board of directors, and employees so they buy into the vision. The more you believe in the vision with a solid conviction, the more influence you will have for people to buy into the vision.

Step 5. Go all in to execute the vision. You only have one life to live on earth!

Offensive Strategy
- Do you have a compelling vision that everyone is willing to go all in to execute?

CHAPTER 6
STRATEGY

> Without consultation, plans are frustrated, but
> with many counselors they succeed.
> —*Proverbs 15:22 (NASB)*

The success of a business depends on how well leadership can influence people to live the purpose, live the values, and go all in to pursue the vision by executing the strategy. To multiply the growth of a business at scale requires building a strategy that can generate leads (marketing), convert leads (sales), and deliver quality product and services in such a way that it can be repeated thousands of times the same way.

Step 1. Surround yourself with wise counselors who are smarter and wiser than you to build your strategy. King Solomon, the writer of Proverbs, was one of wisest humans to live on planet earth (1 Kings 4:30). He recognized that plans succeed with the consultation of multiple counselors and don't work out well without multiple counselors.

Most businesses hire a board of directors with different backgrounds, experiences, and skills to develop the strategy with the collective genius of all the members of the board. It doesn't matter the size of your business or organization, you should invest in a board of directors. If you can't afford to pay for a board of directors, create a virtual team of advisors that you find a way to compensate for their time, knowledge, and experience. I have accountability partners, advisors, and coaches for each area of my life to help shape the decisions I make and navigate tough challenges.

Step 2. Ask the right questions with the right people to get the right answers that align with your purpose, values, and vision. Example of the right questions to ask:
- How will you raise capital to invest in your business?
- How and when will you pay back your investors?
- What is your exit strategy?
- What are the current and future trends that will impact your business?
- What products and services will you deliver?
- How will you differentiate your products and services?
- Who will you partner with to supply you with the components for the products and services?
- What is the market?
- What are the barrier costs to enter the market?
- Who is the competition?
- How viable is the future of the business?
- How will you protect your business from risks?
- How will you price your product and service?
- What is your revenue target?
- What is your profit margin target?
- How will you reinvest the profits?
- How will you compensate your team?
- How will you generate leads?
- How will you convert leads?
- How will you deliver your product and service?
- How will you scale your business?
- How will you organize the business?
- Who will run the business units?
- What are the roles and responsibilities of each business unit?
- Who do you need to hire, and how much do they cost?
- How many people do you need to hire?

- Who will develop the processes for each business unit?
- What are the daily, weekly, monthly, quarterly, and annual rhythms of each business unit?
- What technology will help you execute your strategy?
- What do you need to outsource that is not a core competency of your business?

Step 3. Develop your Business Offense Game Plan. The purpose of the game plan is to help every employee visually see how he or she connects with the purpose, values, vision, and strategy of the business by allowing him or her to create a quarterly game plan aligned with the overall business game plan.

Visit businessoffense.com to download the PDF version of the Business Offense Game Plan and learn where to purchase the print version of the Business Offense Playbook.

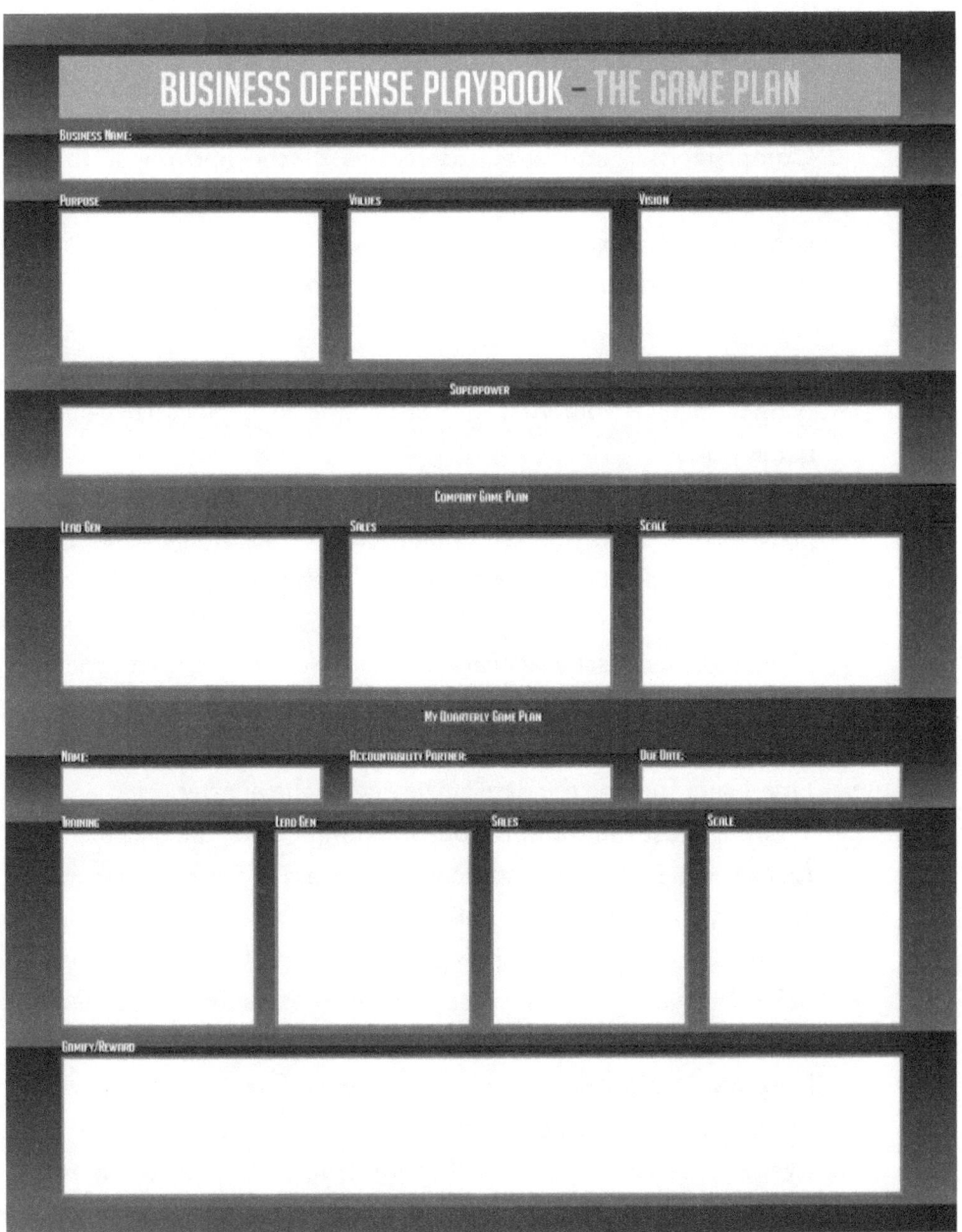

Business Offense Game Plan Worksheet

Leadership team process:
- Complete the top section: business name, purpose, values, vision, and superpower.
- Complete the middle section with the annual goals/targets for these areas: lead gen, sales, and scale.
- Complete the gamify/reward section at the bottom of the business offense game plan to incentivize your employees to execute the strategy.
- Save and share the document with everyone.

All employee process:
- Complete your my quarterly game plan section.
- Name: Include your first and last name to personalize your game plan.
- Accountability: Include the person you will share this game plan with to hold you accountable to execute the game plan. You will need to schedule a meeting with your accountability partner to explain your game plan, seek feedback, adjust the plan, and then start executing the plan. You should invite your accountability partner to check in on your progress at least one time per month.
- Due Date: Include the date at the end of the quarter.
- Training: List the training you will complete for the quarter.
- Lead Gen: List your lead generation targets for the quarter. Even if you are not in marketing or business development, you can help generate leads for your company.
- Sales: List your revenue targets to convert leads for the quarter.
- Scale: List the most important activities you will perform to help your business scale during the quarter. Examples: product/service delivery, business operations, and acquiring companies.
- Leaders: Schedule time with your team to guide them to complete their "my quarterly game plan" section. You can use your completed my quarterly game plan section as an example to your team on how you plan to execute the company strategy.

- Save your business offense game plan to a place on your computer you can easily find.
- Print out your business offense game plan, and post it somewhere you will see it every day to stay focused.

Step 4. Develop you score card to track your game plan performance. You can have the greatest strategy or game plan on planet earth, but if you don't score the strategy, you won't know if you are getting better or worse. The Bible says it this way: "Know well the condition of your flocks, And pay attention to your herds" (Proverbs 27:23 NASB). You have to pay attention to the performance of your strategy by the numbers. The saying "run the business by the numbers" applies to all businesses regardless of size because every business must generate revenue and make a profit to stay in business.

Step 5. Adjust your business offense game plan every quarter. The purpose of your quarterly game plan adjustment is to include the right people to ask the right questions to build an action plan to execute the next quarter. The "right people" can be anyone in the organization or outside the organization you trust to provide valuable feedback and can help you move the business forward. You want to ask the "right questions" to narrow the focus of the action plan. The action plan should focus on generating leads, sales, and scale while making the work fun and exciting. I recommend blocking off one day per quarter somewhere with no distractions and good food to ask the right questions.

BUSINESS OFFENSE PLAYBOOK – GAME PLAN ADJUSTMENTS

What Are The 3 To 5 Most Important Things We Learned About Our Execution In The Past 90 Days?

What Are The 20% Of Activities That Will Generate 80% Of The Results In The Next 90 Days?

How Can We Make Work Fun And Reward Employees For Performance In The Next 90 Days?

Business Offense Game Plan Adjustments Worksheet

Game plan adjustment process:
- Complete the top section by asking: What are the three to five most important things we learned about our strategy in the last ninety days?
- Complete the middle section by asking: What 20 percent of activities will produce 80 percent of the results in next ninety days?
- Complete the bottom section by asking: How can we make executing our strategy fun with prizes, gifts, parties and incentives to build strong teams and promote cooperation?

Step 6. Recover fast when you fail. We live in the real world where everyone will fail at something in business and in life. Most successes in life are birthed from past failures. The second business I launched was a failure, I've had several businesses ideas that were failures, and I've failed to close several big deals for my MSP business. It's not a matter if will you fail but how fast you recover from your failure.

Offensive Strategy
- Do you have a business offense game plan?

CHAPTER 7
FOCUS

Set your minds on things that are above,
not on things that are on earth.
—*Colossians 3:2 (ESV)*

The word focus means the center of interest or activity and the state or quality of having or producing clear visual definition. The definition doesn't say the center of interests or activities. Why? You can only focus on one thing at a time. God didn't design us to focus on multiple things at one time. For example, think about how face-to-face communication works. It's hard to listen to someone speak if we are speaking at the same time. When we listen to someone else speak, we process what he or she says, then we speak, the other person listens, and he or she processes what we say. Each person is in a state of either speaking or listening.

I hardly ever watch TV but used to watch cable news shows. I remember when I watched those types of shows, it sounded like a bunch of noise when they would bring on guests to debate a topic. Everyone was trying to speak or even yell at the same time without listening, which might be one of the reasons why Washington, DC, is so jacked up. What do you think?

In our busy culture, we think we must multitask to get more done, but that's not true. For years, I thought I had to multitask to get ahead, but I was wrong. The attempt by humans to multitask is a dumb idea because that's not how we are wired.

I have a good example of why multitasking is a dumb idea. Raise your hand if you have ever dropped your phone in the toilet or know someone who dropped their phone in the toilet. Please put your hand down now. Thank you for focusing on answering that question. I will be the first to admit that I dropped my phone while peeing and texting at the same time. My hand-eye coordination was not as good as I thought, and neither were my multitasking skills any good.

The last time I checked, the toilet serves one purpose for humans. Now for animals that's a different story because they may get thirsty and take a drink from the water. I am pleased to report that I've never dropped my phone or iPad in the toilet while sitting on the throne reading in peace and solitude. I focus on each step of that process, if you know what I mean.

I started the first chapter of the book writing about the most important relationship in our life, which is our vertical relationship with God. The number-one focus in our lives should be to focus on doing the will of God. Why? We were created by God on purpose for a purpose, so we should focus on living that purpose day by day. The best way I've learned to focus on doing the will of God is to invest time right after I wake up to thank Him, praise Him, ask Him for wisdom, and surrender my will to His will. Throughout the day I pray and recite memorized scripture to keep me focused. Second, I will focus on how I can invest time with my wife. Third, I will focus on how I can invest time with my kids. I try to focus on my relationship with God, my wife, and my family before the workday starts so that I've made them more important than work. Fourth, I will focus on what I need to get done for work.

God created us on purpose for a purpose on this earth to live for Him, which includes solving problems in our businesses, organizations, and communities. If you have a dry-cleaning business, your purpose is to dry clean clothes to save people time of doing clothes themselves. If you have a waste management business, your purpose is to dispose of waste while protecting the environment. If you have a plumbing business, your purpose is to keep water flowing without leaks. If you have a MSP, your purpose is to serve as the IT department for a business or organization.

When we know our purpose, we can focus step by step to live that purpose. Most companies that scale focus on what they are great at and eliminate what they are not great at. They focus on what's going to produce the highest return of output.

If you apply the eighty/twenty rule to a business or organization, then 20 percent of the activities will produce 80 percent of the revenue. Why do you need to perform the 80 percent of the activities that is not generating much revenue? The answer is you don't. If your business currently performs five activities then you would identify the one activity that is producing the 80 percent of the revenue then outsource or eliminate the four activities that are not generating revenue. When you do this, you narrow your focus on the one thing that produces most of the revenue. For my MSP business, we focus on delivering one result, IT certainty, with our IT Offense superpower. I will speak more about superpower in the next chapter.

The process to identify the 20 percent that produces the most results must be a rhythm of your business or organization at least one time per quarter. We tend to think we have to do more to get more results, but that's not true. The key is focusing on what produces the most results and eliminate everything else like it's cancer.

I list what I must get done in the morning of every day, prioritize what is the most important, and then focus on each important item one at a time. There are some days where I will focus on one thing in the morning and then focus on one thing in the afternoon. There are some weeks that I will focus on completing one thing for that week, and all my activities are focused on that one thing. There is not a one-size-fits-all plan strategy but rather a mind-set to focus on one thing at a time.

To better understand the power of focus, I highly recommend reading the book The One Thing: The Surprisingly Simple Truth

Behind Extraordinary Results by Gary Keller and Jay Papasan to gain a clear perspective on the power of focusing on one thing at a time.

Offensive Strategy
- Does your business focus on the most important things that will multiply the growth of the business?

CHAPTER 8
SUPERPOWER

And He has said to me, "My grace is sufficient for you, for power is perfected in weakness." Most gladly, therefore, I will rather boast about my weaknesses, so that the power of Christ may dwell in me.
—*2 Corinthians 12:9 (NASB)*

BUSINESS SUPERPOWER

The beauty of capitalism combined with the internet is that more people can start a business from scratch and compete in the global market. As more people start businesses offering similar products and services, those products and services becomes commoditized. According to Meriam-Webster, the term commodify is to render (a good or service) widely available and interchangeable with one provided by another company. In other words, more and more companies enter the market selling the same products and services, so every company appears to offer the same thing.

One of the most common ways people try to compete in a commoditized market is to offer a lower price than the competition, which forces the competition to find different ways to compete like driving out cost of their business to lower their price, automate, or bundle loss leaders with products and services to increase value.

The greatest example in 2017 is the ongoing war between Amazon and Walmart for customers. Both companies leverage economies of scale to sell the most products on planet earth at the lowest prices. You can purchase most of the same products at Walmart that you can purchase at Amazon for about the same price. Amazon started out selling books online in the late '90s and has developed into selling everything anywhere on the planet. Amazon still sells products and services direct from the internet but also sells directly from brick and mortar stores. Walmart started out selling all types of products at the lowest price from retail brick and mortar stores. Walmart has developed their brick-and-mortar footprint worldwide to sell products and has developed their internet platform to compete head to head with Amazon. It appears that both companies are working toward a similar strategy to offer products and services online and at brick-and-mortar stores.

The key question to ask is which company will you purchase products and services from if they offer the same product at the same price with the same delivery date? More than likely you will purchase from the company with the unique value proposition you trust. The unique value proposition is how a company differentiates products and services from the competition.

I started using the term superpower after hearing Gary Pica, CEO of TruMethods, use this term because it sounded much cooler than "unique value proposition." Your superpower is how you differentiate your products and services in the market so clients have a why to purchase products and services from your company. One of Amazon's superpowers is their Prime Subscription service that you pay an annual or monthly subscription fee to receive additional services like free two-day shipping on eligible products. For my first MSP business, Xccelero, we built our superpower IT Offense to differentiate how we deliver technology products and services and why you should purchase technology products and services from us. Everybody in our industry offers proactive managed services at a fixed fee, but nobody in our business has an IT Offense superpower.

DEFINITION

a. the act of solving IT problems fast
b. the means or methods of aligning IT strategy with business strategy
c. the act of proactive IT management
d. ability to deliver turnkey IT solutions on time and within budget

Our superpower is a combination of people, processes, and technology working together to deliver one result: IT certainty. The result of our superpower is driven by focusing on executing our purpose, values, vision, and strategy and not comparing ourselves to or worrying about the competition. The one result we deliver to clients positively impacts their business in multiple ways:

- Data is protected.
- Employees stay productive.
- Unpredictable costs are avoided.
- Technology risks are reduced.

The process to execute our superpower is a continual cycle that requires executing daily, weekly, monthly, quarterly, and annual rhythms. Our goal is to build our superpower so that we can replicate it five thousand times. If we can replicate it five thousand times, the next step is to replicate it fifty thousand times. If we can replicate it fifty thousand times, then the next step is to replicate it five hundred thousand times. We essentially want to make our superpower our scarce resource that nobody else has since we are a service delivery company.

In economic terms, the scarcer a resource becomes, the more valuable it is in an economy. The less scarce a resource becomes, the less valuable it is in an economy. When more competition enters the market selling the same products and services, the less scarce and valuable the products and services become in the economy.

You should invest in building your superpower like it's the scarcest resource in the economy to build up your value and separate yourself from the competition.

Offensive Strategy
- Are you investing in building your business superpower to separate yourself from the competition?

PERSONAL SUPERPOWER

I believe we were created by God on purpose for a purpose. We have the ability to choose to live our God-inspired purpose or our own purpose. If we live our own purpose, we are ultimately telling God, "I don't need you and can do life with my own talents, strengths, and experience." When we live our God-inspired purpose, we are worshiping God by doing what He created us to do instead of what the world says we should do. The world operates by the survival of the fittest where only the strong and most powerful will survive. The strongest companies survive. The strongest countries survive. The strongest people survive, etc. There is nothing wrong with building a strong company, strong country, or strong body, but the strong things in this world are finite. The kingdom of God operates on this earth by humble, broken, and weak people submitting to the will of God. The Bible says God chose the weak things of the world to shame the strong and the foolish things of the world to shame the wise (1 Corinthians 1:27). Throughout the Bible, God demonstrated His power working through humble, broken, and weak people to accomplish His purposes. The Bible even says that God laughs when kings and rulers plot against His plan (Psalm 2).

Paul was dispatched by God to preach the gospel to the Gentiles and suffered more than anyone else except for Jesus. Paul was a tough dude, strong in his faith, having survived being beaten with rods three times, stoned one time (not by marijuana but by rocks), shipwrecked three times, hungry, and imprisoned. In 2 Corinthians 12, we learn that Paul had a vision of the third heaven and to keep him humble, God used a messenger from Satan to torment him. Paul, a tough dude, strong in his faith, pleaded with God three times to stop the torment. God responded to Paul in 2 Corinthians 12:9-10 (NASB),

> And He has said to me, "My grace is sufficient for you, for power is perfected in weakness." Most gladly, therefore, I will rather boast about my weaknesses, so that the power of Christ may dwell in me. Therefore I am well content with weaknesses, with insults, with distresses, with persecutions, with difficulties, for Christ's sake; for when I am weak, then I am strong.

Nick Vujicic was born without arms or legs in 1982 in Melbourne, Australia, without any medical explanation or warning. Can you imagine going through your daily routine without arms or legs? Think about the basic functions you do every day, like bathing, eating, changing clothes, etc. It would be a very challenging way to live. Nick struggled throughout his childhood, wondering why he was different from all other kids and questioned the purpose of life. However, Nick responded to the gospel message, was saved, and started following Jesus. Nick discovered his purpose was to start a global ministry called Life without Limbs to share the hope and love of Jesus with the world. Jesus gave Nick the strength to do what could be considered as impossible but with God nothing is impossible (Luke 1:37).

We can build our own personal superpower with our talents, strengths, and experiences, but we can't even breathe without God allowing the breath. God is looking for humble, broken, and weak people who will submit to His will by faith so He can demonstrate His superpower through their lives. If you want to realize your true personal superpower, live and walk by the spirit of God in humility, boasting in your weakness to allow God's power to flow through your weaknesses.

Offensive Strategy

- Are you living and walking by the spirit of God in humility, boasting in your weakness?

CHAPTER 9
LEAD GEN

> To Him who led His people through the wilderness,
> For His lovingkindness is everlasting.
> —*Psalm 136:16 (NASB)*

The internet has enabled more businesses than ever the ability to compete. The increase in competition generates an increase in choices for customers to select from in the market. The increase in choices causes products and services to be viewed as commodities, thus making your lead-generation strategy essential to multiplying the growth of your business. Lead generation is the process of attracting new customers to purchase your products or services by articulating your unique value proposition aka superpower. Please understand there is no one-trick pony when it comes to lead generation. You must consistently invest time, money, and effort in multiple lead-generation tactics to break through the noise, build creditability, and stay top of mind in the market to attract new clients.

IDENTIFY YOUR TARGET MARKET

The process of building your lead-generation strategy starts with identifying your target market by completing these steps:

Step 1. Discover who will buy your products and services based on demographics, type of customer (consumer or businesses), and location.

Step 2. Decide if you want to sell to a horizontal (broad) market, vertical (narrow) market, or multiple vertical (narrow) markets. The broader the market you go after, the more likely you will have a lot of competition and price compression. The narrower the market you go after, the more you can invest in learning that market and focusing on specific messaging for that specific market. However, your business success will depend on the success of the vertical market you focus on. If that vertical market goes extinct, so will your business. Most businesses that scale offer multiple products and services to a broad market or multiple vertical markets to diversify their revenue streams, similar to how investors diversify investing capital in multiple funds or businesses.

Step 3. Analyze the competition, barrier costs, risks, and ROI to determine if it makes financial sense to pursue the target market.

Step 4. Document your target market, and communicate your target market to your team.

BUILD CREDIBILITY

Now that you have identified your target market, you need to build credibility for your target market by employing these proven tactics:
- Become an expert in the target market.
- Have customer reference accounts in the same markets.
- Create customer case studies for the markets.
- Write or contribute to articles for industry publications.
- Attend industry trade shows and events for the target market.
- Read trade news and journals for the target market.
- Learn the markets terms and concepts to "speak the language."

EDUTAIN

The entertainment business is one of the easiest businesses to scale fast because humans are visual creatures who love to be entertained and expect to be entertained. The term edutainment is a combination of using education, humor, and entertainment to attract people to your business. If you can combine education, humor, and entertainment in a quality-produced video, you are more likely to break through the noise online to attract people to your business. You will need to commit to produce ongoing quality edutainment content to continue to build your followers and maximize the effectiveness of generating leads from this strategy.

GO PUBLIC

One of the most effective ways to raise awareness to your business is to release press releases. A press release is essentially a way to invite the media to give you air time to gain attention. The best practice to go public is to hire a public relations expert to help you with this process. A public relations expert will know what to say, who to send the press release to and how to maximize the effectiveness of the press release.

NETWORK SMART

My grandfather and father both advised me at an early age to network with people. When I started my first business, I tried to network everywhere I could to meet as many people as possible to generate the most leads as possible but quickly learned that my efforts didn't deliver the ROI I expected. I decided to focus on networking smarter by focusing on only attending networking events that included customers in my target market, centers of influence, people in my power base, and people that I may want to hire to avoid wasting time, energy, and effort on events that would not generate any leads.

PICK UP THE PHONE

In the modern era of digital technology and online media, it's easy to forget the most effective tool in a lead-generation arsenal is the telephone. Whether you call from a soft phone, Skype app, FaceTime app, mobile phone, VOIP phone, or analog phone, you can reach virtually anyone on planet earth. The inside sales process is still an effective lead-generating system to incorporate in your business. Everyone is providing eBooks, publishing blog content, sending newsletters letters, posting on social media, but inside sales worked before the modern digital era. How do inside sales work? Inside sales work like sifting for gold. You have to sift through all the rocks and debris to find the gold by making a massive number of calls.

In 2017 there were 260 business days assuming a five-day work week. If the average employee takes two weeks for vacation, eight paid days off, and eight federal holidays, he or she is working 234 business days per year. If you multiply 234 by eight hours a day, you have 1,872 working business hours. If you apply the eighty/twenty rule, assuming an employee is only productive six hours a day, you have 1,497 production hours. If you hire an inside salesperson to make a minimum of 10 calls per hour, that is 60 calls per day or 14,040 calls per year.

When you make inside sales calls, you need to have the mind-set that prospects are expecting to receive your call because you offer the best solution in the market. When you get rejected, smile, update your CRM, and then immediately make the next call on your list. The purpose of the inside sales call varies by the type of business. In the SaaS world, you may call prospects multiple times before you are able to schedule a demo or offer a free trial. If you stay positive and persistent, you will be successful. In the MSP world, you call prospects to gather information to update in your CRM and set up an appointment to meet in person. Unless the prospect is in immediate pain, it may take multiple phone calls before you are able to set up an appointment. As you are making calls to prospects, you are building your internal lead gen database because every call has value.

We used the inside sales process below in my first MSP to build our internal lead gen database while trying to set up appointments for our outside sales team.

1. Pick up the phone and call businesses loaded from the marketing list in the CRM!
2. Gain first time-appointments for outside sales.
   a. Assign first-time appointments as an activity in CRM to outside sales team.
3. Every call has value. Update CRM with:

    a. Contact name and email address
    b. Count of client devices, servers, backup storage
    c. Line of business applications
    d. Current IT support model
    e. IT support contract end date
 4. Classify the business in CRM
    a. Suspect—business doesn't know who we are
    b. Prospect—business knows who we are
    c. Not a fit—business is not a fit for our service
    d. Under contract—business is under contract with another MSP
    e. Outside sales—handed off to outside sales team

From an accountability perspective, it's best to leverage a CRM system that enables you to assign points to activities to sum up the total activity points for performance incentives that you can track last week, week-to-date, month-to-date, quarter-to-date, and year-to-date. For example, we encourage our inside sales team to generate 550 activity points per week based on the activity point table below. If an inside salesperson generates 50 calls per day times 2 points times 5 days, it equals 500 points. The remaining 50 points can easily be made up with the other available activities listed in the table. The activity point system will help drive the behavior of your inside sales team when they know daily how they are performing toward achieving their activity points goal.

Activity	Points
Appointment	5
Ask for sale	10
Call	2
Demo	10
Email	1
Follow-up	2
Marketing	3
Quote	5
Renew agreement	10

PICK UP THE PEN

It's hard to replace the thoughtfulness of picking up a pen to write a handwritten note to thank, honor, or praise someone. A handwritten note goes a long way toward building relationships with people because you demonstrate you are thinking of them and willing to invest time in the relationships by writing a handwritten note. I recommend blocking off time each month to write handwritten notes to customers, prospects, and people in your power base and then follow up with them to make sure they receive the note. You will be surprised over time by the fruit you bear from this lead-generating strategy.

SEND SNAIL MAIL

Sending snail mail can be an effective lead-generating strategy if you are willing to follow up with each person you send a direct mail package to verify he or she received the mail and ask him or her for the opportunity to meet in person to discuss what you sent. Sending direct mail essentially gives you a premise to call a prospect to follow up.

Snail Mail Process:
1. Decide on the campaign
2. Proofread material
3. Identify list
4. Budget
5. Create follow-up tracking system in CRM
6. Order packaging
7. Order postage
8. Create labels
9. Print labels
10. Drop off mail at post office
11. Follow-up using list in CRM
12. Call each company that received mailer to ask for appointment
13. Hand off to outside sales

SPEAK LIKE A PRO

When you demonstrate expertise on a subject, you attract opportunities to speak about your expertise. One of the reasons I wrote this book was to demonstrate expertise in multiplying the growth of businesses with people, process, and technology to get speaking engagements either in person, on TV, on live broadcasts, or in online media. In most cases, you will start getting opportunities to speak to small audiences and then build up to larger audiences over time. Regardless of whether you write a book or not, you will need to develop a presentation to demonstrate your expertise aka *superpower*. I recommend creating the presentation following this process:

- Presentation development
    - What content relates to the audience and will keep them engaged?
    - How will you use humor in the presentation?
    - Where will you encourage participation?
    - How much time margin will you create to answer questions at the end?
    - Has someone proofread the presentation to check for errors and verify it will relate to the audience?
    - Who will go with you to support you, connect with participants, and answer questions?
- Preparation
    - Have you rehearsed the presentation? As a general rule one minute of presentation time needs one hour of preparation.
    - Have you created a checklist to verify what you need to bring?
    - What is your follow-up process after the presentation?
- Presentation
    - Dress for success
    - Arrive early
    - Rehearse presentation

- Remember high energy and humor wins to keep your audience engaged.
- Giveaway
  - Collect business cards at beginning of presentation for a giveaway at the end.
- Audience Participation
  - Facilitate participation by asking questions for audience participation.
  - Provide an envelope with a gift card and free consultation.
  - Collect participate information to follow up.
- Follow up
  - Follow up with participants after the presentation.

BUILD A SHOPPING CART

Everyone understands how to purchase a product or service online, but not every business leverages shopping carts to promote or sell their products and services. A shopping cart can be used as a lead-generating tool by promoting your products and services with "learn more" or "buy now" buttons on social media sites and including links to buy your products and services in email campaigns. You don't have to be an Amazon, Walmart, Best Buy, etc., to have a shopping cart. You can set up a shopping cart by investing a few hundred dollars up front and then invest a monthly fee to subscribe to services like Shopify to host your shopping cart and use Mail Chimp to promote your shopping cart via email and social media campaigns.

ADVERTISE SMART

Advertising works differently for each type of business and may or may not generate leads for your business. For example, car dealerships advertise heavily on radio and TV because they want to influence you while you are driving via radio and while you are watching TV at home. A dental practice may advertise via paid social media advertising to reach a specific demographic in their area instead of a radio or TV campaign. The great thing about digital advertising is you can easily track the results to capture your return on investment. McDonalds invests millions of dollars to market to all demographics but also specializes in marketing to children with its Ronald McDonald and Happy Meal campaigns.

You may have to invest in a combination of advertising to a broad market with a broad message and advertising to vertical markets with specialized messages to break through the noise and scale your lead-generation strategy.

KNOW YOUR NUMBERS

If you rely only on word-of-mouth or referral marketing, you will limit the potential growth of your business. To make money, you have to invest money, and to run a business, you need to know your numbers, including lead generation. The two key lead-generation numbers you need to know are:

1. How many leads does it take to acquire a new customer per the lead-generation process?
2. What is the cost per lead per lead-generation process?

The cost per lead will be different for each lead-generation process you incorporate in your business. You need to know your cost per lead-generation process so you can forecast the amount of money you need to invest to execute your overall lead-generation strategy. For example, if you know that you have to invest $10 in lead-generation for every $100 in revenue you can forecast how much money you need to invest. If your revenue goal is $30 million, you will need to invest $3 million in lead generation.

Offensive Strategy

- Do you have repeatable lead-generation processes in place where you understand the costs and measure the results?

CHAPTER 10
SALES

A false balance is an abomination to the LORD,
But a just weight is His delight.
—*Proverbs 11:1 NASB*

The key to sales is to believe in what you are selling, commit to sell your product or service, and never give up. If you don't believe in your product or service, you shouldn't sell your product or service. Why? You will not be able to sustain the commitment required to be successful. A great example of someone believing in his product, committing to sell his product, and never giving up is Harland David Sanders.

Harland David Sanders (a.k.a., Colonel Sanders), twenty-five-year-old restaurant business failed when he was sixty-five years old, which left him with very little money. He could have given up and retired, but instead at age sixty-six, he focused on selling his chicken recipe to restaurants for several years which, eventually led to the creation of Kentucky Fried Chicken. As you know, KFC is one of the most well-known restaurant franchises in the world because Colonel Sanders believed in his chicken recipe, committed to sell his recipe, and never gave up. What is even more interesting about this story is that God never gave up loving Colonel Sanders, and at age seventy-seven, Colonel Sanders responded to the real love of God by trusting Jesus as his Lord and Savior!

ACCEPT REJECTION

You may be the greatest salesperson in the world, but you will get rejected. Rejection is part of life and part of the sales process, so accept it, embrace it, and move forward without fear. If you are not getting rejected every day, you are probably not generating the right amount of action to be great at sales. You must have a positive mental attitude, courage, and a relentless drive to never give up being successful in sales.

BUILD TRUST

The number one reason people purchase a product or service is they trust the value they will receive from the product or service. For example, let's say you want to purchase a tumbler to keep your drinks cold. You go to your local store to purchase a tumbler and notice several different brands of tumblers on the shelf. You look at the price of a Yeti tumbler versus a cheaper knock off brand. If you purchase the Yeti you trust the value of the Yeti brand over the knockoff brand at a lower price. If you purchase the knockoff brand at a lower price, you really don't trust the price of the Yeti matches the value. The reason products and services go on "sale" is to influence you to trust you are getting a great deal to purchase the product or service.

In business-to-business selling, you may have to engage prospects five to fifteen times before they will trust you to purchase your product or service. The process of building trust requires repetition. The reality is the prospect is receiving tons of sales calls, emails, social media posts, direct mail, etc., from your competition. You have to separate yourself from the competition so your prospect buys in to the value you provide with your product or service before they will buy your product or service.

INVEST IN SALES TRAINING

Your sales force and employees are like knives. They might be sharp for a season, but if you don't continue to sharpen the knives with training, they will get dull. The more your sales team invests in training on the products and services you offer, your sales process, industry trends, and role-playing, the more potential your business has to multiply. The most effective sales training is role-playing. I recommend you role-play with your sales team to prepare for each sales meeting with a prospect and even existing client. You want to role-play for the common objections and questions the prospect may ask so you are prepared to go into the meeting and close the sale. Now sharpen your knives, slice through objections, and close sales.

ASK THE RIGHT QUESTIONS

A colleague of mine, Chris Atkinson, developed a list of ten questions specific to the vertical market he focused on to ask every prospect he met with to identify opportunities. The key to sales is asking the right question to help you identify pain.

The more questions you can ask, the more you likely you will keep the prospect engaged in the sales process, and more opportunity, you will have to identify pain. In my MSP, we frame questions based on what is important to the prospect, what does it mean to the prospect if x happens, how does the prospect respond if x happens, and what is the impact if x happens. We created twenty general questions to identify IT pain points. We don't ask each prospect the twenty questions but focus on asking a few questions from the list based on the conversations we've had with the prospect to speak directly to their pain.

Business continuity question:
- What is the impact to your business if your critical servers fail or you discover you are unable to restore data because your backup systems were not working?

Internet connectivity question:
- What is the impact to your business if your employees are unable to access cloud applications and servers or process credit card transactions when your internet connection goes down?

Cyber security questions:
- What is the impact to your business if your systems and data are comprised from a cyber-attack?
- What is the impact to your business if you are audited and they discover you didn't implement the required policy, process, and procedures?
- Is it important for you to do business with a company that implement systems and controls to protect against and respond to cybersecurity threats?

Network connectivity questions:
- What is the impact to your business when your network runs slow or is not reliable?
- What is the impact to your business when employees spend time searching the internet for non-related business purposes and downloading unauthorized or pirated software?
- What is the impact to your business when you have to manage, support, and replace different wireless and wired networks?
- What is the impact to your business when your free guest Wi-Fi isn't working?

Voice communication question:
- What is the impact to your business when you have to pay multiple telecom companies for local and long distance?
- What is the impact to your business when you have to manage, support, and replace your on-premises telephone equipment?

Technical support question:
- What is the impact to your business when your current IT provider is unavailable to help your business?
- What is the impact to your business when your current IT provider doesn't send certified or properly trained staff to support your environment?
- What is the impact to your business when your current IT provider fails to live up to their promises?

- What is the impact to your business when your current IT provider sends you a bill higher than what you expected?
- What is the impact to your business when your current IT provider doesn't properly document systems or follow standard operating procedures?

Why outsource IT vs. hire internal IT resource
- What is the impact to your business when IT staff takes vacation, is out sick, or is on extended leave and you don't have backup IT support?
- How do you respond when IT staff run out of projects or challenges and start looking for a new job?
- How do you respond when IT staff are offered a higher salary?
- What is the impact to your business if IT staff leaves without fully documenting the environment?

BUILD THE PROPOSAL

The first step in building a proposal is to confirm you can meet in person or video conference to present the proposal. If the prospect is not willing to invest time to listen to your proposal, then you shouldn't invest time building the proposal. The second step is to understand you will be price shopped. You will not close every sale, and thus there is no point in wasting time creating custom proposals for every opportunity.

The best practice to streamline the proposal creation process is to build workflows that guide your sales team to select proposal templates with prebuilt packages that solve common pain points. As you discover new pain points, you can add those as prebuilt packages to the templates. If you do have to create a custom proposal that requires a lot of time, you may want to consider charging the prospect for your time up front and then deduct what they paid up front from the proposal cost if they accept the proposal.

PRESENT THE PROPOSAL

The purpose of presenting the proposal is to lead the prospect to a yes or no decision as fast as possible to shorten the sales cycle. The longer it takes to close a sale, the longer your businesses waits to generate new revenue to multiply your business.

Most people want to know how you're different from the competition, how your solution will solve their pain points, how much will it cost, how much time it will take to implement, what are the terms/conditions, and what are the risks. Everything outside of those basic questions is noise, so there is no point wasting time presenting a lengthy dog and pony show. Your presentation should answer all the questions and include an agreement ready to be signed.

The presentation process is an opportunity to not only lead the prospect to a yes or no decision but to improve your presentation skills reading people and learning on the fly. For example, I presented a proposal to the executive team of a very successful electrical contractor. The VP of operations told us he didn't care about the pigments; he only cared about the color. In other words, he cared about the end result of the solution we were proposing to his company, not all the ingredients, feeds, and speeds. My belief in selling the end result, IT certainty, was reaffirmed, and I gained an illustration to use while presenting to other prospects. I used the color end result illustration while presenting to a new prospect by asking, "What is your favorite color?" Then I asked, "Do you care about the color or the pigments?" The purpose was to tell them that we take care of the pigments so you only see the color or the end result. On one occasion, I had one prospect, Pastor Morgan Golden ask me, "What if my favorite color is plaid?" and all I could do was bust out laughing because I was caught off guard by the cleverness of the question. We were able to convert that prospect into a client!

HANDOFF

The next step after receiving money for your product/service or a signed agreement is to hand off the sales order to the product and service delivery team without dropping the ball. In football, the quarterback and center snap exchange is critical to the quarterback being able to execute a run or pass play. If the center or quarterback mishandles the snap, the play won't get executed, the ball could be turned over, and even the game could be lost depending on the situation. The sales team is like the center that hands the ball off to the product/service delivery team that executes the play (a.k.a., process to deliver the product/service).

FOLLOW-UP

Never assume the handoff between the sales team and product/service delivery team will go smoothly even though that should be the expectation for every transaction. Always follow up with each client after selling a product/service to verify they received exactly what they were sold and address any problems swiftly to maintain trust with your client. Schedule regular follow-ups after the sale to maintain trust in the relationship.

STIMULATE SALES

The best way to stimulate sales growth is to offer generous incentive programs that are easy to understand to all your employees. Every employee in your company, regardless of role, has the potential to sell your product/service to someone he or she knows. Your employees need to know what the incentive is, how they can achieve the incentive, and when they will get paid for the incentive to stimulate sales growth from all your employees. You want to keep the incentive programs fresh and exciting for your employees. In addition, you should go big with your sales incentives throughout the year to challenge your employees to sell more.

PRICING

The first thing most of us do to test the market for a product and service is to open up a web browser on our smartphone, tablet, or computer to search the internet for the best price, which can cause us to think we have to match or lower our price to compete for the products and service we sell, but that's not always true. When you price your product and service, you need to focus on the net profit you will generate from the sale of each product and service. The net profit is what enables your business to reinvest in your business so you can improve your business and scale your business, which helps your current and future clients.

I know the temptation is to lower the price to compete, especially in a market with a lot of competition, but this is where your superpower kicks in. When you focus on building a superpower for your business that enables you to deliver better products and services, why would you lower your price or match the competition's price? You shouldn't lower your price or match their price but probably raise the price if you are providing better value.

The traditional method of formulating your pricing is to determine your cost of goods sold and cost of sale for the product/service, evaluate the pricing on the market, and then determine your price. It's definitely smart to know what the competition is offering and how much they charge for their product and service, but you need to invest more time in building your superpower. You didn't start your business to sell your competition's product and services but to sell your products and services. You can price yourself out of business by charging too much as well as not charging enough.

KNOW YOUR NUMBERS

As mentioned in the lead-generation chapter you need to know your numbers to forecast acquiring new customers. In terms of sales, you need to know two key numbers:

1. What is the average time required to close each sale?
2. What is the average cost required to close each sale?

The average cost and time it takes to close a sale for an online or retail purchase is less than a traditional business to business sale.

For example, the average time to close a business-to-business sale should include the time on the phone calling the prospect, traveling to meet with the prospect, building the proposal/statement of work, face-to-face meetings with the prospect, following up via email, reviewing the terms and conditions with the prospect, obtaining a signed agreement, generating a sales order, processing the sales order, and following up. The average cost to close a business-to-business sale should include the cost of time, sales materials, meals and entertainment, gas, salary, and commission required to close the sale.

Offensive Strategy
- Do you have a repeatable sales process in place that you understand the costs and measure the results?

CHAPTER 11
SCALE

Commit your works to the LORD And your plans will be established.
—*Proverbs 16:3 (NASB)*

Why do you want to scale your business? One word: thrive. It's difficult to make it in current economy and/or future economy with increased competition and price compression without scaling your business. The process of scaling a business is like building a software application with people, process, and technology. You start with why you are building the app (purpose), what behaviors/actions the app will perform (values), and the roadmap of the app (vision). Next you hire a team of business process experts, UX designers, developers, and project managers to use a software development cycle to build the app and release the app (strategy). You can quickly clone additional copies of the app fast for almost no additional incremental cost, which is ideally how you want your business to scale.

LEARN FROM THE FOUNDER OF THE UNIVERSE

What do you think a being with an infinite mind could do if man with a finite mind is able to scale large empires, businesses, and organizations? My friend Jamie Clifton asked me one day, "What does the word universe mean?" I said I don't know. He said, "The word uni means one and the word verse means sentence." He then asked, "How did God create the heavens and the earth?" The answer to Jamie's question is located in the first book of the Bible. The Bible says God created the heavens and the earth by speaking sentences (Genesis 1). The first sentence He spoke was, "Let there be light," and there was light (Genesis 1:3).

God created and scaled 100 billion–plus galaxies and 100 billion–plus creatures from His Word, but God created man in His image and likeness by forming him from the dust of the ground and then breathed the breath of life into Adam, making him a living being (Genesis 2:7). He created woman by putting Adam to sleep and removing a bone from his rib cage and then formed her out of the bone (Genesis 2:21–22). From that one breath He breathed into Adam, God created and scaled the entire human population. The ability we have to scale a business or do anything in life comes from the one breath God breathed into Adam. Yes, God is so powerful that He only needed to breathe one time into Adam to create 100 billion–plus humans who have lived on planet earth.

Does it make sense to you to learn how God wants you to live and find out what your purpose is on this earth since He has created and scaled the universe with His word and breathe?

LEARN FROM THE FOUNDER OF MCDONALDS

The book eMyth Revisited teaches the principle of scaling a business by systemizing the business in such a way that it can be replicated five thousand times and the five thousandth unit would run as smoothly as the first. The most well-known example of systemizing a business is McDonald's. Ray Croc purchased the McDonald's franchise in 1961 for $2.7 million from the McDonald brothers. Ray had a vision to multiply the growth of McDonalds but started slow, demanding consistency in the quality, service, and cleanliness of the operation. Ray's grill man, Fred Turner, created Hamburger University in 1961 to train franchise owners how to operate a McDonald's store. As of 2017, there were seven Hamburger Universities located worldwide and thirty-six thousand McDonald's operating in one hundred countries. The key to success of McDonald's is that they created a plug-and-produce system where anyone could be trained to perform any task at a McDonald's restaurant to produce the consistent results.

PLUG AND PRODUCE

The term plug and play originated from the ability of Microsoft Windows to automatically detect new hardware and install the driver software to enable the new hardware to work in the computer

Plug and play has come a long way over time as Microsoft has refined their frameworks for vendors to follow to build compatible hardware, and the computer industry has refined standards to make hardware more plug and play. The process took tens of millions of dollars, thousands of people, and years to make plug and play work like it does today.

In business, you want to create a plug and produce system based on defined roles and responsibilities, repeatable processes, business rhythms, and training so that when you hire new employees, you can plug them into their role to start executing repeatable processes and business rhythms.

HIRE SMART

The key to building a plug-and-produce business is to hire smart by recruiting and finding the right people who can plug into your business offense. The term right people means matching up people to defined roles and responsibilities based on their past performance and potential for future performance.

The first way to hire smart is to cultivate relationships with your talent base, as discussed in chapter 1. The people in your talent base are people who you know their character, competency, and potential to weave into the fabric of the business. I like to hire people in my talent base to perform contract work so I can test their abilities before making an offer to hire them full time. This saves a lot of time and avoids the expense of hiring someone you think can do the job but actually can't do the job, and you have to let him or her go.

The second way to hire smart is to build a business that attracts people to come work for your business. The more people attracted to work at your business, the more potential your business can cost effectively acquire new talent to plug into your business offense. A great strategy to attract talent is to use social media to showcase the culture of your company. The cooler and more exciting a place is to work, the more likely you will be to attract top talent.

The third way to hire smart is to ask people you trust who they would recommend for a position in your business. You have to be careful that someone is not trying to kick the can down the road, so to speak, by praising someone they want you to hire because they don't have the courage to fire them.

The fourth way is to recruit via advertising, online job boards, expos, job fairs, and college campuses to broaden the number of candidates you have available to select from to hire. Regardless of the method you use to recruit new hires, you need a process to select new hires and onboard new hires. I included the processes from my first MSP as examples below to use in your business.

HOW TO SELECT TECHNICAL NEW HIRES

1. Search for candidate
2. Pre-interview screening
   - Review resumes to identify the top five resumes that closely match the job positing.
3. Schedule interviews of the people with the top five resumes.
   - Ask if they have noncompete agreement with their current employer.
4. Perform face-to-face interview.
   - What adversity have they experienced?
   - How do they handle failure?
   - How do they handle frustration?
   - What are their top three to five accomplishments in IT?
   - How do they sharpen their technology skills?
   - How many computing devices do they have at home?
5. Perform second face-to-face interview with hiring manager and team.
6. Perform background and reference check.
7. Final questions to ask before making decision to hire:

Character
- Do they have a teachable spirit?
- Do we believe they will live the purpose and values of our business?

Competency
- Do we believe they have the will and skill to execute their role in the business strategy?
- Do we believe they will be an asset?

Chemistry
- Do we believe they will "weave" into the fabric of our business?

8. Notify candidates of decision within forty-eight hours after decision is made.
9. Hire candidate on ninety-day trial.

HOW TO ONBOARD NEW HIRES—COMPANY RESPONSIBILITIES

1. Complete essential documentation
    - Send employee offer letter via Adobe EchoSign.
    - Send employee manual via Adobe EchoSign.
    - Send W4 form to employee via Adobe EchoSign.
    - Send I9 form to employee - Employee Eligibility Verification.
    - Request picture of driver license.
    - Store essential documentation in ERP.
2. Register with state's new hire reporting program.
3. Complete employee payroll and benefits packet.
4. Set up employee benefits.
5. Set up scorecard based on role.
6. Provision and assign tools.
7. Order gear.
8. Take new hire to lunch with team.
9. Leadership to communicate purpose, values, vision, strategy, expectations, and scorecard.
10. Market new employee to clients.

HOW TO ONBOARD NEW HIRES — EMPLOYEE RESPONSIBILITIES

1. Learn our business rhythms and tools.
2. Learn our proactive admin standards.
3. Learn how to use our documentation platform.
4. Learn how to access our blueprints.
5. Complete ERP system training.
6. Complete RMM system training.
7. Complete cybersecurity system training.
8. Complete BDR system training.
9. Complete firewall training.
10. Complete cloud PBX training.
11. Complete cloud server training.
12. Complete quoting tool training.
13. Get to know client environment in documentation platform.
14. Schedule meeting with leadership to complete business offense game plan.

ROLES AND RESPONSIBILITIES

The purpose of clarifying roles and responsibilities is to avoid employee frustration and eliminate redundancy and ambiguity in a business. When employees are plugged into defined roles with defined responsibilities, they gain certainty for what they are expected to do, the goals they are expected to achieve, and how they help execute the overall business strategy.

The leadership team can build repeatable processes for the roles, train employees consistently on how to execute the processes of their role, and hold employees accountable to meet performance standards for their role. When all roles and responsibilities are defined, the possibility of two departments working on the same function is eliminated, thus preventing redundancy and waste in the business.

BUILD REPEATABLE PROCESSES

The first step to build repeatable processes is to find out if you can reuse an existing process instead of reinventing the wheel, which is exactly what I did when I wrote my first book The Hurry Up No Huddle Life Offense. I purchased and read the book APE: Author, Publisher, Entrepreneur written by Guy Kawasaki and Shawn Welch. In APE, Guy and Shawn guide you through the process of writing and publishing a book. The book served as a repeatable process that enabled me to write my first book and publish the book online with the potential to scale the sales of the book globally. I could have invested countless hours to build my own process to write and publish my book, but I was able to write it and publish in less than eight months thanks to learning from APE. Ray Croc's commitment in the early years of McDonald's to build and execute repeatable processes led to McDonald's operating thirty-six thousand stores worldwide as of 2017. McDonald's franchise owners don't have to reinvent the wheel or build their own process but rather leverage the proven, repeatable process from McDonalds and training provided by Hamburger U.

Leveraging proven repeatable processes and best practices is like leveraging software code and apps in the open source movement. There is no reason to reinvent the software code if it's available and relevant to what you are trying to automate.

You will not always be able to reuse a process and will have to build your own process. You may have guessed this already, but there is a process to build a process. You ideally want to automate as many processes as possible and use a workflow to guide people to execute nonautomated processes.

Step 1. The process to build a process starts with asking these following questions:
- Why do we need the process?
- What is the opportunity cost building the process?
- What is the expected end result of the process?
- Do we have the right people helping us build the process?

- How will the process be executed?
- When will the process be executed?
- Where will the process be executed?
- Who will execute the process?
- Who will inspect the process was executed?

Step 2. The process to build a process requires refining the process by asking these questions:
- Can we remove any steps from the process?
- Can we easily train people to execute the process?
- If we change this, what will be the impact?
- If we don't change this, what will be the impact?
- What does it mean to our people?
- What does it mean to our clients/customers?
- Can we automate the process?

Step 3. The process to build a process requires testing the process, measuring the results of the process, and then deciding if it's ready to release the process for production.

Step 4. The process to build a process requires training people to execute the process.

Step 5. Release the process in production, score the performance of the process, and commit to continuously improving your process.

CONTINUOUS IMPROVEMENT

In business, if you keep doing something that is not profitable, your business will die. In football, if you keep executing the same offensive plays, the defense will eventually be able to stop you, and you will probably not win many football games. Regardless of the business size, every business must invest time, money, and resources to continuously improve its operations. Continuous improvement should be ingrained in the culture of your people by reviewing processes every quarter and encouraging employees to find a better way with incentives.

The world moves fast. Your business will change and your customers will change, which means you must adjust your processes to stay competitive in the current and future economy. I don't recommend changing what is currently working or changing your process for the sake of change because if you have a lot of change all the time, it can cause complexity in your business and slow you down.

If you're steering a big ship at sea and make a hard turn, you can wreck the ship. The same is true for business. If you try to aggressively steer your business in another direction without buy-in from your team, training, and a process to handle it, you can wreck your business.

BUSINESS RHYTHMS

How does your team execute what they need to do consistently when they are pushed and pulled in different directions every day? The simple answer is to leverage business rhythms. A business rhythm is a recurring operation that is performed on a daily, weekly, monthly, quarterly, or annual basis to guide your team to execute consistently. When your team knows what they are expected to do, when they are expected to do it, how they are expected to do it and why they are expected to do it, your business will operate like a symphony orchestra creating a beautiful melody. Your business will deliver results consistently and move faster than the competition because you essentially automate your team.

The easiest way to model your business rhythms is to use a Spreadsheet, Google Doc, or Microsoft SharePoint list. In my MSP, we leveraged Microsoft SharePoint to create one central repository for all our business rhythms. We use the Microsoft SharePoint view feature to create views for each business rhythm to help guide our team in what they need to execute consistently on a daily, as needed, ongoing, weekly, monthly, quarterly, and annual basis. We are able share one link to the business rhythms repository to all employees so they can select the business rhythm view by frequency and then drill down by function, role, and role category.

The business rhythm repository helps visualize the who, what, where, when, why, and how with clearly defined roles and responsibilities by business function. We can use the repository to analyze what we can automate, streamline, outsource, improve, or eliminate from our operations. We populate sixteen columns in our business rhythm repository as shown in the table below:

Column	Purpose of Column
Frequency	How often do we need to execute this rhythm? Example: Daily
Day of the Month	What day of the month do we need to execute the rhythm? Example: Week day
Execution Order	What is the order to execute the rhythm? Example: One to indicate it should be done first
Function	What is the business function of the rhythm? Example: Sales
Function Owner	Who is responsible for the business function? Example: VP of Sales
Role	What is the role of the business function responsible to execute the rhythm? Example: Inside sales
Role Category	What is the category of the role responsible to execute the rhythm? Example: Dials
Role Owner	Who is responsible for the business role? Example: Inside sales rep
Process	What is the process for the rhythm? Example: Make seventy calls per day
Process Instructions	What are the instructions to execute the process? Example: We recommend creating videos along with concisely documented steps to guide your team.

System	What is the system/technology used with the process? Example: Sales Force
Time	How much time will it take in minutes to complete the rhythm? Example: 360 minutes
Metric	How will we measure the performance of the rhythm execution? Example: Seventy dials
Reward	What is the incentive/reward for achieving the metric? Example: 140 Activity Points
Automated	Is the rhythm automated? Example: No
Outsourced	Is the rhythm outsourced? Example: No

Ideally, you want to automate as many rhythms as possible to scale your business fast and to execute fast, but you can't automate everything. You can simplify how to execute nonautomated tasks using the business rhythm system, and building guided workflows and processes to help employees execute consistently.

DAY OF THE WEEK THEMES

Pete Carroll, a championship-winning coach in college and the NFL, is known for creating a theme for each day of the week to focus his football teams on specific areas. Coach Carroll started the days of the week themes in the '90s to seize the day.

We included his days of the week theme posted on the Seattle Seahawks September 7, 2010, blog below:

> "Tell the Truth Monday" • The team discusses the pluses and minuses from the previous game so that they "can

move forward together and be clear with what needs to be worked on," Carroll said.

"Day off Tuesday" • Players receive a break from workouts, meetings and other team-related activities, per NFL off day rules. This is the main day the Seahawks make their mark doing charitable appearances in the community.

"Competition Wednesday" • Coaches and players turn the focus inward on the hardest practice day of the week. "It's all about competition on this day," Carroll said. "It's about us and getting us right by practicing our tails off."

"Turnover Thursday" • The offense stresses taking care of the football while the defense focuses on taking away the football during the practice, with both sides fighting for the day's "victory." "Our No. 1 emphasis is taking care of the football," Carroll said. "This day lets us get back to our philosophy of 'it's all about the ball.' It's dedicated to getting after and protecting the football."

"No Repeat Friday" • The goal for the day is to be so precise that no plays in the brief practice need to be repeated or reviewed. "We want to make sure everything is just right and that we get everything exactly the way we want it for the game," Carroll said.

"Review Saturday" • After three days of intense practices, the team tapers down to a final review on the day before the big test. Meetings and the brief walk-thru are geared toward fine-tuning and running through the game plan.

"Game day Sunday" • The previous six days of preparation come together for the final product on Sunday afternoon. "You win the game by the way you prepare through the week," Carroll said. "If you prepare your best, you put yourself in position to play your very best in the game."

We loved Coach Carroll's days of the week theme so much we created our own days of the week theme at Xccelero to guide our team to maximize their daily production.

Start Fast Monday
- People start slow when they come back to work after a weekend. They take their time and make excuses because it's a Monday. The goal for Start Fast Monday is to arrive to work engaged, prepared, and fired up to attack the challenges during the week. We don't have time to make excuses that it's a Monday!

Today Not Tomorrow Tuesday
- People think they can push out rhythms, activities, or tickets scheduled for Tuesday since there are three more days in the week, but that just delays executing a rhythm, solving client problems, or gaining a new client. The goal for Today Not Tomorrow Tuesday is to execute everything we can on Tuesday and only push out what we don't have time to complete.

No Complacency Wednesday
- People refer to Wednesday as the hump day where performance peaks and then starts slowing down the rest of the week. The goal of No Complacency Wednesday is to not get comfortable that it's the middle of the week but instead get excited to execute our rhythms and complete our activities and tickets.

Stay Hungry Thursday
- People generally start slowing down their work performance on Thursdays. The goal of Stay Hungry Thursday is to speed up

our performance by staying hungry to execute our rhythms and complete our activities and tickets.

Finish Strong Friday
- People start disengaging from work on Fridays to look forward to the weekend. We finish the week strong by executing all weekly rhythms and completing all outstanding activities and tickets scheduled for the week to set up our team to Start Fast Monday.

EXECUTE FAST

The new currency in the world is speed. The businesses that can move fast with people, process, and technology to generate leads, convert leads, and scale their operations are in the best position to multiply. The businesses that move at turtle speed, don't innovate, and are not able to scale will probably go out of business.

I knew when I started my company, Xccelero, we had to execute fast, innovate, and scale fast to stay in business. The name Xccelero means "execute fast." The first two letters XC is short for execute and celero in Latin means fast. At Xccelero, we execute fast to help businesses execute their vision with people, process, and technology.

Offensive Strategy
- Do you have a plug and produce business that can execute fast and scale fast?

CHAPTER 12
CYBERSECURITY

Do not fear, for I am with you; Do not anxiously look about you, for I am your God. I will strengthen you, surely I will help you, Surely I will uphold you with My righteous right hand.
—Isaiah 41:10 (NASB)

This chapter will help you understand why you need a comprehensive cybersecurity strategy and how to implement a cybersecurity strategy.

HUMAN FIREWALL

The most important component of your cybersecurity strategy is the human firewall. The human firewall is only as strong as how well your people are trained to mitigate cybersecurity threats. The best practice to train your people is to subscribe to a security awareness training program from companies like EC-Council, KnowBe4, Webroot, SANS Institute, CERT.org, and many others.

The investment in security awareness training should not be something you remove as a line item for your budget but consider to be a high priority to protect one of your business's most important assets: data.

Offensive Strategy

- Are you investing in a security awareness training program to build up your human firewall?

DATA

Data is the information your business or organization stores in digital format that can be electronically transmitted and processed. Data should be protected and secured like it's one of the scarcest resources in your business. When you deposit money in the bank, do you expect the banking institution to implement processes, controls, and safeguards to protect your money from being stolen? Do you expect the banking institution to implement processes, controls, and safeguards to prevent people from hacking into your account to discover how much money you have and your transaction history? I believe we all agree the answer is yes.

The data of your business is not only a scarce resource but also like a currency of your business. Your business data is circulated internally and/or externally like the flow of money circulated within an economy. The economy depends on the flow of money in exchange for goods and services, and your business depends on the flow of data to enable employees to deliver goods and services to customers. If your money is stolen, you will have less money in circulation to buy goods and services. If your data is damaged or stolen, you could potentially lose customers, thus directly impacting the amount of revenue flowing into the business. The point of this illustration is to change your perception to invest in securing your data assets like a bank invests in protecting monetary assets.

As technology becomes easier to use, more data is generated and stored in centralized cloud/SaaS applications and decentralized like tablets, laptops, and smartphones. The ability to secure and back up data centralized in the cloud or decentralized on a device becomes more challenging. The best practice is to implement policy, process, and controls to centralize data as much as possible to limit where you must safeguard and back up data.

Offensive Strategy
- Write down a list of all locations your business data is being stored, and then ask your team, "How is your data being safeguarded in each of these locations?"

BACKUP AND DISASTER RECOVERY

The second line of defense in your cybersecurity strategy is implementing a backup and disaster recovery system to protect your business data wherever it lives. Your business data can live inside your company's on-premises infrastructure or outside your company's on-premises infrastructure, like in the cloud or an offsite location. Regardless of where the data lives, it should be backed up with a simple way to recover the data because disasters normally occur at the most inopportune times. Before I started my MSP, I worked for a company as regional IT manager responsible for managing IT operations over a multistate footprint. My footprint expanded and was given a new location and staff to manage. The first thing I discovered during my site review was there was no backup process in place to back up the file servers at the location. I had to scramble to come up with backup hardware and software to implement a backup and disaster recovery process for the location.

While we were waiting for the hardware to arrive, my IT person had planned to go on a family vacation. The day he left for vacation, the primary file server at the new location failed. This server contained the budget files the finance team was using to develop the expense and capital budgets with a very tight deadline. We had no backup in place, and thus we couldn't recover the files, so I had to call my IT person and ask him to come back to the office to fix the problem. Otherwise I was going to have to dispatch another team member in a different state to drive to the location to fix the problem.

He drove back to the office, discovered a RAID Array controller failed, replaced the part, and booted up the server with no data loss, and the finance team finished their budgets.

The first mistake businesses make is not having a business-grade backup and disaster recovery solution in place. The second mistake businesses make is not verifying the backup and disaster recovery process and system works. The best practice is to select a solution that offers automated backup verification, point-in-time backups replicated to an on-site appliance, and a cloud data center with 24–7 support.

In addition, you want to reduce your recovery time by selecting a solution that can restore data and virtualize backed-up servers within minutes. I recommend staying away from the low-cost solutions for your business and especially staying away from performing backups to a rotation of removable hard drives.

Offensive Strategy
- Have you verified your backup and disaster recovery solution works?

PHYSICAL

There are two main components to physical security: facility security and workspace security. Facility security is how your business secures access to equipment with data, and workspace security is how each employee secures his or her workspace. There are many ways to secure a facility, from armed guards, drones, robots, video surveillance, access control systems, and basic lock and key. Whatever system your budget can afford, you need to make sure you have controls in place to authorize who has access, when they have access, how to monitor access, and what to do if there is a security breach. The likelihood of someone breaking into your facility to seize equipment with data is a lower risk than someone from inside of the organization stealing, destroying, or leaking data.

Workspace security starts with employees securing their office environments by following these practical steps:
- Don't leave removable media lying around your desk with company data.
- Don't leave your computer logged in when you are away from your desk. Most IT departments and MSPs implement policies to cause the screen to lock after a specified period of inactivity.

- Don't leave written or printed usernames and passwords around your desk. There are several applications available to help you securely store usernames and passwords, so you don't need to write them down.
- Don't leave documents that contain sensitive information on your desk. File or shred the documents securely when finished reviewing the documents.
- Shred documents with sensitive information before disposing of them in the trash.
- Lock and close file cabinets.
- Don't leave keys or access control cards on your desk.
- Don't leave IDs, credentials, credit cards, or purchase cards on your desk.
- Use privacy screens to prevent someone from looking over your shoulder to view what you are working on your computer.

Offensive Strategy
- Is your business following physical security best practices?

AUTHENTICATION

You may have built a fort as a kid and required your friends to provide a secret password to enter the fort. If a kid decides to share the secret password with other kids the password is no longer a secret, and thus anyone can gain access to the fort unless the password is changed.

This is the basic concept to an authentication system: a device or user requests access to a resource, a system verifies access to a resource and then grants or denies access based on if the device or user has access to the resource. If someone gains the authentication credentials to the resource, he or she can share the credentials with anyone to gain access to the resource. This is the reason why using two-step authentication mechanisms is so important in the cloud age. Two-step authentication verifies the who that has access to the what. For example, when you access services like Office 365, anyone with Internet access can use your credentials to access your Office 365 services. When you implement two-step authentications, Office 365 authorizes who is trying to access the what by sending a text to your cellphone, calling your phone, or sending an email to a secondary email address with a random generated code that you enter to confirm you are the legitimate owner of the first set of credentials entered.

Offensive Strategy
- Do you have a two-factor authentication system to protect access to your IT systems?

EMAIL

Email is one of the most-used technologies on planet earth, which makes it one of the most vulnerable to a cybersecurity attack. The number one email cybersecurity attack is a Phishing attack. Cyber criminals want to "fish" for your sensitive information or influence you to click a link that will run malicious code on your computer to gain access to your computer.

The most common phishing attacks are:
- Embedding links into emails that redirect users to an unsecured website requesting sensitive information.
- Installing Trojans via a malicious email attachment.
- Spoofing the sender email address in an email to appear as a reputable source and requesting sensitive information.

The best practice to mitigate phishing attacks is to do the following:
- Don't reveal personal or financial information in email.
- Pay attention to the URL.
- Check the security of the website the email link is trying to redirect you to.
- Verify suspicious email requests.
- Notify your MSP or IT department if you have questions or believe your email is part of a phishing attack.
- Implement anti-spam and end point security software to protect your email system and computers with email access.

In addition to phishing attacks, employees may send out confidential information via email by accident or on purpose. Sending email across the internet is like placing a hundred-dollar bill in a clear plastic envelope and mailing it cross country via the Postal Service. Everyone who handles the mail will easily see there is a hundred-dollar bill in the envelope. The same is true for email. When you send an email from one email server to the next email server, the email by default is not encrypted and can be read by anyone with the right tools/skills as it traverses the internet.

If the email is encrypted, the email is uploaded from the sending email server to the encrypted mail server. The destination email address receives a code to authenticate to download the encrypted email.

The best practice to protect outbound email communication is to do the following:
- Communicate to employees what they can/cannot send out via email.
- Use email encryption to send out anything they may be considered confidential.
- Implement data loss prevention technology to scan the email system to protect against confidential information leaking through the email system.

Offensive Strategy
- Do you have a strategy in place to mitigate inbound and outbound email cybersecurity threats?

WEBSITE AND SOCIAL MEDIA
Suring the web and accessing social media is virtually the daily routine of billions of people on planet earth, which is very appealing to cybercriminals. Cybercriminals create schemes to deceive people and exploit software vulnerabilities in software applications and operating systems.

The most common web and social media cybersecurity threats are:
- Malvertising
- Social media scams

- Click hacking
- Fake pages
- Web-based exploits

The best practice to protect against web and social media threats is to do the following:

- Be conservative about what you download, and be careful with everything that is free. Why would someone write sophisticated software code and give it away for free? What is the hook?
- Interact with only well-known websites.
- Beware of antivirus scams that pop up a message "we detected a virus" or "click this link to download the antivirus software."
- Access web and social media sites through a firewall to filter and scrutinize web and social media content.
- Tunnel DNS traffic from inside a corporate network to a third party like Open DNS to filter and block access to known malicious websites.
- Deploy end point security software that automatically checks websites in the browser and prevents access to known malicious sites.

Offensive Strategy

- Have you implemented the best practices for web and social media access?

MOBILE

We live in and will continue to live in a mobile-first, cloud-first world, as Satya Nadella made famous in his 2014 press briefing after taking over at Microsoft. A mobile device is anything you can take with you outside of your business network that contains data, such as: wearables, watches, smartphones, tablets, and laptops.

The most common mobile cybersecurity threats that can jeopardize business data are:

- Lost, misplaced, or stolen devices.
- Mobile malware.

- Unsecure third-party apps.
- Files with sensitive information accidently emailed to an unauthorized party or posted online.

The best practice to protect mobile devices against cybersecurity threats is to do the following:
- Create a standard way to configure mobile devices.
- Set pin or passcode with auto screen lock.
- Use remote locate tools.
- Use mobile device management agent software.
- Use encryption.
- Keep devices clean by carefully selecting what you download.
- Perform regular audits to verify your configurations align with your standards.

Offensive Strategy
- Do you have a strategy in place to mitigate mobile cybersecurity threats?

CLOUD

The internet has enabled great innovation and communication but has also opened the door to the potential of being hacked by amateur hackers learning how to hack systems reading information on the internet to sophisticated cyber criminals or nation states developing software program like bots to probe and scan IP addresses for open ports that may have a way into a network. For example, a cybercriminal could write a software program that reads the information from your website to gather the list of employees at your business assuming you publish that information on the website. The program could then perform a query in DNS to gather the IP addresses of your mail, web, or other cloud servers. Next the program could scan for open ports of common protocols like Outlook Web Access and Remote Desktop Protocol to try to login with random passwords entering the employee names harvested from the external website. This can all happen in a matter of seconds with the speed of technology. The good news is most of these types of attacks can be prevented with firewalls and intrusion-detection systems.

Not only are you subject to external hacking when you expose services in the cloud, but you are also subject to someone easily deleting data in the cloud if you don't have the controls and backup systems in place to safeguard and protect your data.

The term cloud can refer to a group of computers on a private network within the walls of a company or on the public network outside the walls of a company. There are private clouds, public clouds, community clouds, and hybrid clouds. A private cloud is set up inside a business that is used internally for that business. A public cloud like Google, Amazon AWS, Apple iCloud, or Microsoft Azure/Office 365 are the general storage and hosting services that are used by businesses or consumers over the internet. A hybrid cloud is generally a mix of private and public clouds. For example, you may host applications on your private cloud that leverage storage in the public cloud to store or backup data. A community cloud like Facebook, Snapchat, or Twitter belongs to a group of organizations or people with similar interests.

The most common cloud cybersecurity threats are:
- Privacy laws are violated due to storing cloud data in a geographical location not allowed by the law.
- Sensitive or confidential information is viewed, stolen, or destroyed by an unauthorized person or application.
- Data is lost due to either no backup systems in place or the backup system doesn't work.
- The credentials to the cloud service are hacked and compromised.
- A disgruntled employee deletes virtual cloud servers, storage, or data or infects cloud servers with malicious programs.

The best practice to protect against cloud cybersecurity threats is to do the following:
- Create a standard way to configure and secure cloud services.
- Verify your cloud data and cloud backups are stored in a geographical location allowed by law.
- Implement cloud backups and verify the backups work.

- Use strong passwords with two-step authentication.
- Encrypt data in the cloud.
- Limit sensitive and confidential data stored in the cloud.
- Perform regular audits to verify your configurations align with your standards.

Offensive Strategy
- Have you thought through your cloud strategy to mitigate cloud cybersecurity threats?

NETWORK CONNECTIONS

A network connection is essentially the way a computing device connects to other computing devices over a wired or wireless medium. Both types of network connections are subject to cybersecurity threats if a computing device infected with malware connects to the network or an unauthorized person gains access to the network to steal or destroy data.

In a wireless network, a computing device doesn't have to physically connect to a network switch with a patch cable, so you don't have to be inside the building to connect to the network. The average radius of a wireless signal indoors is 150 feet and outdoors 300 feet. A wireless network can pose a greater risk than a wired network if the wireless network is not configured properly to authenticate access to authorized devices and segment network traffic between guest and business networks.

In a wired network, an employee can simply plug in a router device from home thinking it will give him or her more ports for his or her office, but the employee doesn't realize the router-issued IP address probably on a different subnet from the business network. The computers on the business network receive the IP address from the home-based router and thus are unable to connect to resources on the business network. The IT department receives tickets people are unable to connect, troubleshoot the problem, and determine another device is issuing IP addresses.

The most common cybersecurity threats to network connections are:

- Not securing physical access to network equipment.
- Not configuring routers, switches, wireless access points, or firewalls in a standard way.
- Not proactively managing the network.
- Not properly labeling network connections.
- Allowing any device to connect to the network.
- Allowing access to the business network via wireless with only a passphrase.
- Not controlling IP address assignment and management from a central device.
- Not controlling or tracking the applications and bandwidth consumed on the network.
- Allowing remote access without two-step authentication, SSL or secure VPN connection.

The best practice to configure and secure network connections is to do the following:

- Create a standard way to configure and secure network connections.
- Label and document all network connections.
- Keep routers, switches, wireless access points, and firewalls updated with the latest firmware and updates.
- Use cloud-managed routers, switches, wireless access points, and firewalls that can provide visibility into network access and behaviors.
- Secure access to the internet with a proactively managed and updated firewall.
- Secure how IP addresses are managed and issued on the network.
- Control wired and wireless network traffic using virtual LANs, access control lists, and time of day limits.
- Use authentication systems to secure access to network resources.
- Perform regular internal and external vulnerable scans.
- Implement threat detection and response technology to monitor activity and generate alerts based on suspicious activity.

- Implement network access control to enforce allowing computing devices that meet specific criteria to connect to the network.
- Require employees who connect remotely to use two-step authentication or VPN.
- Perform regular audits to verify your configurations align with your standards.

Offensive Strategy
- Have you secured the network connections at your business?

OPERATING SYSTEM AND APPLICATION LOCKDOWN

The operating system is the brain of all computing devices and typically is the most complex software running on a device. The more complex software is, the more potential cybercriminals can identify and exploit security vulnerabilities. Virtually every piece of software written has flaws (a.k.a., bugs) when the software is launched to the public, which is why it's important to lock down the operating system and applications that run on top of the operating system.

The most common cybersecurity attacks related the operating system and applications are:

- No standards in place to configure the operating system and applications.
- No controls in place to limit what applications can run on the operating system.
- Granting everyone local administrator rights.
- Malicious code is not detected by the end point security software.
- The latest updates and security patches are not applied to applications or the operating system.

The best practice to lock down the operating systems and applications is to do the following:

- Inventory what applications each department needs to run to do their job.
- Create a standard way to configure operating systems and applications.

- Create a standard operating procedure for how to install the operating system and applications.
- Limit local administrator access to prevent installing unauthorized applications.
- Limit what applications can run on computers using mechanisms such as software restriction policies in Microsoft Group Policy.
- Run applications in a virtual or remote desktop environment.
- Deploy end protection software.
- Deploy remote monitoring and management software to:
  - automatically install the latest updates and patches to the operating system and applications.
  - automatically schedule maintenance tasks and scripts to prevent problems or further lockdown the operating system or applications.
  - automatically generate alerts and tickets when problems arise.
  - automatically inventory the applications and operating systems installed.
- Perform regular audits to verify your configurations align with your standards.

Offensive Strategy
- Do you have a strategy in place to lock down the operating system and applications?

INCIDENT RESPONSE

The last cybersecurity strategy component mentioned is the one that most people forget about. Every business needs a process to handle what to do when a security incident happens and who to report the security incident to after discovering the security incident. The first step is to always notify your IT Department or MSP as well as executive management so they are aware. In some businesses, you may be required by law to report the incident, and it may be least expensive on the front end to hire a lawyer to identify your responsibilities and help you develop a plan to mitigate risk, including creating an incident response plan.

Offensive Strategy

- Do you have an incident response plan?

CHAPTER 13
TECHNOLOGY ROAD MAP

> In all your ways acknowledge Him, And He
> will make your paths straight.
> —*Proverbs 3:6 NASB*

This chapter will help you build a technology road map by engaging with the right people, discovering opportunities, improving the IT environment, driving IT innovation, and accelerating the business with information technology.

ENGAGE

A business doesn't exist to align with the technology strategy, but technology exists to align with the business strategy. The process to build a technology road map starts with engaging people who understand the business strategy and vision.

Step 1. Meet with business leaders to learn about the business strategy and vision.

Step 2. Gain the trust of business leaders, demonstrate you respect their time, and treat them as partners to move the relationship into a partnership.

Step 3. Continue to build the partnership with the business leaders, technology champions, and other stakeholders through positive relationship building, following up, meeting expectations, and communicating and coordinating.

DISCOVER

The discovery process consists of learning how the people, process, and technology currently align with the business strategy and vision.

Step 1. Learn the key information about the business to gain a high-level understanding of the business strategy and how IT is currently aligned with the business strategy.
- What is the business strategy and vision?
- What services does the business provide, and who is their target market?
- What are the top business priorities?
- How is the organization structured?
- How many locations do they have?
- How many employees does the business have?
- Who are the key vendors and partners?
- What are the industry, state, or federal regulations that impact the business?
- What are the top IT pain points?
- How and when do employees receive cybersecurity and technology strategy?
- How do business units use technology?
- How and when do business units want to receive change updates, problem updates, and IT strategy updates?
- Who needs to be involved with planning the technology strategy/roadmap?

Step 2. Learn the key IT processes of the business to gain a high-level understanding of the IT operations.

Strategic Planning
- What is the annual capital and expense budget for technology?
- What is the process to manage the IT budget?

- What is the process to forecast future needs/expansion?
- What is the process to procure hardware, software, and contracts?
- What is the process to train employees in how to use technology?
- What is the process to train the IT team in how to use new technology and execute processes?
- What is the process to measure IT performance?
- What is the process to communicate IT updates/strategy to business units?

Reactive Support
- How do business units receive tech support?
- Where can business units find how-to documentation, knowledge base, and training videos?
- What is the current service level agreement?
- What are the support hours?
- How are support requests communicated?
- What are the average response and resolve times?
- What tools does the IT team use to provide reactive support?

Proactive Administration
- What standards and best practices are in place to manage the IT infrastructure?
- How often is the IT infrastructure audited to align with the standards and best practices?
- How is the IT infrastructure and related components documented?
- What does the IT team use to manage and monitor the IT infrastructure?

Project Delivery
- What is the process to intake new projects?
- How are projects prioritized?
- How are projects planned and executed?
- How are project changes managed and approved?

Step 3. Learn how the key IT infrastructure is implemented in the business to gain a high-level understanding of what can be standardized, streamlined, and optimized.

Cybersecurity
- How often do employees receive security awareness training?
- What systems are in production to safeguard data?
- What backup and disaster recovery systems are in production to protect data and keep systems up?
- When is the last time someone verified the backup and disaster recovery systems works?
- What systems are implemented to protect physical access to locations that contain business data?
- What authentication systems are in production to authorize access to IT resources?
- What systems are in production to protect inbound and outbound email communication?
- What systems are in production to protect internet, web, and social media access?
- What systems are in production to protect mobile devices?
- Where is cloud data/services hosted at, and how are they protected?
- What systems are in production to protect network connections?
- What systems are in production to lock down the operating systems and applications?

Network
- What is the primary internet connection?
- What is the secondary internet connection?
- Is the current network fast enough?
- What methods are in production to segment and prioritize network traffic?
- What methods are in production to gain visibility into network traffic?

- How do employees access the network remotely?
- Does the network infrastructure have the following in production?
  - Network equipment excluding wireless access points deployed in secure rooms that are clean with climate/humidity control
  - Network management software
  - Network equipment connected to battery backups
  - Standardized network equipment
  - Cloud managed firewalls, routers, switches, and wireless access points with active subscriptions
  - Power over ethernet
  - Network connections run from jack to network switch
  - Network connections are labeled
  - CAT E5e or higher wiring
- Do you have spare network equipment, cables, jacks, and other related parts available?
- What is the expected lifecycle of a network device?

Telephony
- Who is the voice service provider, and what services do they offer?
- Are the current voice services under contract?
- What voice services are in production?
  - VOIP from Cloud PBX
  - SIP Trunks
  - Voice from telephone company
  - Voice from cable company
  - Fiber, T1, T3, or MPLS
  - Fax
  - Toll free
  - Direct inward dialing
- What are the local telephone numbers?
- What are the toll-free telephone numbers?

- What local number does each toll-free number route to?
- What is the make, model, and count of telephone in production?
- Do you use power over ethernet for the IP phones?
- Do any telephones have side cars for additional buttons?
- Are the phones owned or leased?
- What is the make and model of headsets in production?
- What is the make, model, count, and location of conference room phones?
- Are soft phones in production?
- What analog devices are in production?
- Do multiple locations use the same phone system?
- Is your phone system premise based or cloud based?
- How are inbound calls routed during business hours and after business hours?
- Does your business have a call center?
- Are you required to record phone calls?
- Does your business route voicemail to email?
- Does your business use video conferencing technology?
- What are all the other features in production for the phone system?
- Do you have spare telephones, headsets, and other related parts available?
- What is the expected lifecycle the phone system?

Servers and Storage
- What is the purpose of each server in production?
- Where are the servers hosted?
- Is every server backed up?
- What are the types of servers in production?
- Do virtual servers have the following in production?
    - Valid license for the OS, server applications, and client access licenses
    - Virtualization software and support licenses
    - Virtualization management software

- Do physical servers have the following in production?
    - Valid license for the OS, server applications, and client access licenses
    - Manufacturer management tools installed
    - Redundant power supplies installed and connected to battery backup
    - Server deployed in secure rooms with climate/humidity control
    - Data is stored on redundant storage arrays
    - Server is under warranty
    - Spare parts are available onsite for mission critical servers
- What is the expected lifecycle of a server?

Clients
- What types of clients and how many clients are in production?
    - PC desktop or laptop
    - Mac desktop or laptop
    - iOS or Android tablet
    - Thin Client
- What client OS is in production by client type?
- Do clients meet the application vendors hardware requirements?
- Do clients have the following in production?
    - Multiple monitors
    - Privacy screens
    - SSD drives
    - Connected to UPS
    - Smart card or biometric
    - Docking stations for laptops
    - Office equipment connected directly to client
- Are employees allowed to store files and data on their client devices or required to store on a server?
- Do you have spare client devices and related parts available?
- What is the expected lifecycle of a client?

Applications
- What is the productivity software in production?
- What are the line of business applications in production?
- Does the line of business applications in production have valid licenses and active vendor support agreements?
- Does the business have custom-built applications? If so, does the business have a copy of the source code with documentation?
- What is the expected lifecycle of the application?

Step 4. Identify how to maximize the investments of current IT infrastructure.

Step 5. Ask the finance department to provide you with the operational and capital expenses for IT and telecom within the past one to three years.

Step 6. Identify opportunities to eliminate expenses and negotiate better terms/pricing with vendors and partners.

IMPROVE

The first areas to focus on improving are the IT processes and infrastructure. Both serve as the pavement on your technology roadmap to enable driving IT innovation. Business leaders normally view IT process and infrastructure improvement as cost centers because they don't understand the impact both of these areas have on the overall IT operations and business.

Step 1. Analyze what your team learned in the discovery process, and then identify the IT processes and infrastructure to streamline, standardize, and optimize.

Step 2. Create the plan to streamline, standardize, and optimize the IT processes and infrastructure.

Step 3. Create a proposal that answers the common questions business leaders will ask:

- Why do we need to execute the plan?
    - Remember, a business is in business to make money. Business leaders are not concerned about the speeds and feeds but the bottom-line impact to the business. The why they should focus on the impact to the business. For example, the why might be:
        - Protect data
        - Keep employees productive
        - Avoid unpredictable costs
        - Lower technology risks
- What is the cost to execute the plan?
- What is the communication plan?
- How much time will it take to execute the plan?
- Who will need to be involved to execute the plan?
- How will you measure the results of the plan?

Step 4. Meet with business leaders to present the plan and obtain buy-in to move forward with the plan.

Step 5. Communicate, coordinate, and follow-up with business leaders to execute the plan.

Step 6. Execute the plan.

Step 7. Measure the execution of the plan on a scorecard.

Step 8. Meet with business leaders on a regular basis to review the scorecard.

INNOVATE

The businesses that fail to innovate normally die because they are not able to keep up with competition that continues to innovate. When you streamline, standardize, and optimize the IT process and infrastructure, you can focus on driving innovation in the business using information technology.

Step 1. Meet with business unit leaders to perform a deep dive discovery of their workflows, how they use technology, and the result they want to achieve. Consider hiring a technical writer to document the current workflow.

Step 2. Analyze the current workflow from the deep-dive discovery process to identify opportunities. Consider hiring a consultant with business analysis experience to help with this step.

Step 3. Assemble people from the business unit, business analysis team, technical writing team, and IT team to collaborate and document the workflow to deliver a new or better result.

Step 4. Perform research to find out if a solution already exists on the market or if a solution needs to be custom developed to implement the new workflow.

Step 5. Obtain approval from business leaders to move forward with a pilot project or outsource building a prototype of the solution to test the use case of the solution.

Step 6. Measure the results of the pilot project or prototype with the team to decide if it's worth investing in the new solution or testing another solution. Repeat steps 4 to 5 if testing another solution.

Step 7. Present the results from the pilot project or prototype use case to business leaders. Obtain buy-in to move forward with implementing the new solution.

ACCELERATE

The world is full of competitors trying to leverage people, process, and technology to take market share from your business. The best way to compete in the current and future economy is to have the mind-set of putting your foot on the gas pedal to accelerate faster using technology.

CHAPTER 14
BINARY

He made Him who knew no sin to be sin on our behalf, so that we might become the righteousness of God in Him.
—*2 Corinthians 5:21 (NASB)*

As simple as this may sound, a computer can only add, subtract, multiply, and divide 1s and 0s using the binary numeric system. Computer data essentially is a string of 1s and 0s:

00011010100110001100010001001000110

01100111001000100010001001001001100

The two-digit binary numeric system of 1s and 0s, the basis for binary code, was discovered by Gottfried Leibniz in 1679.

> Leibniz believed that binary numbers were symbolic of the Christian idea of creation out of nothing. Leibniz was trying to find a system that converts logic's verbal statements into a pure mathematical one.
>
> In computing and telecommunications, binary codes are used for various methods of encoding data, such as character strings, into bit strings. Those methods may use fixed-width or variable-width strings.

> In a fixed-width binary code, each letter, digit, or other character is represented by a bit string of the same length; that bit string, interpreted as a binary number, is usually displayed in code tables in octal, decimal or hexadecimal notation. There are many character sets and many character encodings for them. A bit string, interpreted as a binary number, can be translated into a decimal number. For example, the lower-case a, if represented by the bit string 01100001 (as it is in the standard ASCII code), can also be represented as the decimal number 97.

In layman's terms, we have discovered a way to make computers process data the way we understand using a two-digit binary system. The 1 represents the onstage of electricity and the 0 represents the off stage of electricity. The computer processes the on and off stages of electricity as the binary code.

The reason I included binary as the last chapter is to explain in laymen's terms that our lives on this earth are binary: we are born, and we die. By now you understand that I intentionally included the gospel message throughout this book because my purpose on earth is to reach people with the gospel message to multiply the kingdom of God and help people reach their God-given potential on this earth, including but not limited to multiplying their business with people, process, and technology.

I'm going to use binary code to help illustrate the gospel message. It only takes one sin to separate us eternally from the presence of God (Romans 6:23). What is sin? Sin is missing the mark of the standard of God. The standard of God is perfection because God is perfect (Matthew 5:48). Why are we held to the standard of God? We are created in the image and likeness of God (Genesis 1:27). Every human being, except Jesus, who has lived, is currently alive, or will live in the future has sinned or will sin against God (Romans 3:23).

Throughout our lives, our sin patterns may look like the binary code below where the 0 represents obeying God's law and the 1 represents sin:

00000000000000000000000011100001111001111111111111111110000111111111111111111111110000000000000111111111111111111000

You may believe that you can earn your way to heaven through good works, whether it's tithing, curing cancer, giving away all your possessions, being a "good person," etc., so your life may look like a long string of good works over sin in binary code where 0 represents good works and 1 represents sin:

000000000000111111111111111111111111110000000001111100000001111111111111111111111111100000000000000000001000000000000010111110000000000010000010000000000100000000000000

You may believe that you can lose your salvation if you fall back into a pattern of sin in your life where the 0 represents living righteously and the 1 represents sin:

00000000000000000000000000000000000000000000000001111111111111111111111111100000000011111111111111111111111111

However, none of this is true because of the one who was sent from heaven to the earth out of love (John 3:16); the one who had his booty wiped by sinners (Luke 2); the one who was baptized (Luke 3); the one the Father called His beloved Son who He is well pleased before He did one work of ministry (Luke 3); the one who defeated Satan in the wilderness with just His word (Matthew 4); the one who healed the sick and cast out demons (Mark 1); the one who forgave sinners (Luke 7); the one who confronted the religious elite (Luke 11); the one who followed the will of Father God precisely (John 6:38); the one who allowed sinners to hammer nails into His body on a wooden cross (Matthew 27) to receive the wrath of God for the sins of everyone who believes (2 Corinthians 5:21); the one who breathed the breath of life to the first Adam (Genesis 2:7) and as the last Adam (1 Corinthians 15:45) breathed His last breath (Luke 23:46) to redeem the breath He gave to the first Adam; the one who God raised from the grave (Luke 24); the one who defeated sin and death (1 Corinthians 15:55–57); the one who can sympathize with our weaknesses (Hebrews 4:14–16); the one who is the same yesterday, today, and forever (Hebrews 13:8); the one who is the way, the truth, and the life (John 14:6); the one who can save you by His grace through faith (Ephesians 2:8); the one who can turn your sin to zero (Hebrews 8:12); and the one whose name is the name above all names (Philippians 2:9). His name is Jesus.

www.ingramcontent.com/pod-product-compliance
Lightning Source LLC
Chambersburg PA
CBHW020437220526
45464CB00002B/737